DARTMOOR

THE THREATENED WILDERNESS

BRIAN CARTER

DARTMOOR
THE THREATENED WILDERNESS

Edited by
BRIAN SKILTON

A CHANNEL FOUR BOOK
CENTURY
London Melbourne Auckland Johannesburg

First published in 1987 by Century Hutchinson Ltd
Brookmount House, 62-65 Chandos Place, Covent Garden
London WC2N 4NW

Century Hutchinson Australia Pty Ltd
PO Box 496, 16-22 Church Street, Hawthorn, Victoria 3122
Australia

Century Hutchinson New Zealand Ltd
PO Box 40-086, Glenfield, Auckland 10
New Zealand

Century Hutchinson South Africa Pty Ltd
PO Box 337, Bergvlei
2012 South Africa

Design by Paul Bowden and Elizabeth van Amerongen
Map by Rodney Paull
Front cover: Bennett's Cross
Back cover: Peter Hannaford at Sherwell Farm

Set by SX Composing Ltd
Printed and bound in the Netherlands by
Drukkerij de Lange/van Leer bv, Deventer

British Library Cataloguing in Publication Data
Carter, Brian
Dartmoor: the threatened wilderness.
1. Dartmoor (England)———Description and
travel
I. Title   II. Skilton, Brian
914.23'5304858   DA670.D2

ISBN 0 7126 1756 6

**Opposite title page: Through a John Bishop wall across Swincombe Valley
to Bellever and the North Moor.**

CONTENTS

FOREWORD

Wordsworth wrote: 'Nature never did betray the heart that loved her'. Yet so often we have betrayed Nature. As a Devonian, Dartmoor is pivotal to my consciousness. It is there among the clouds above the place where I live; and the wilderness continues to offer consolation and beauty throughout the seasons, year after year.

In the light of humanity's recent mistakes and transgressions, I cannot help fearing for the place. We are so careless with the world and the rest of creation, and wilderness like Dartmoor is rarely weighed for its own worth. The shadow of the dodo falls across everything touched by humanity and, because the Moor is my heart-place, I care for it passionately, and only ask that it be left alone for others to enjoy in the future as I enjoy it now.

This book is a celebration of a landscape. If anything, it represents a loner's vision, a vision that is shared by my friend and colleague, Brian Skilton. I hope we have provided a voice for the voiceless.

Brian Carter
May 1987

OKEHAMPTON
Sticklepath
South Tawton
Cheriton Bishop
Belstone
South Zeal
Taw
Okehampton Camp
Belstone Tor
Whiddon Down
Drewsteignton
Meldon Quarry
Cosdon Beacon
Spinisters Rock
R. Teign
Meldon Reservoir
Sourton Tors
Yes Tor
Throwleigh
Fingle Bridge
Black Tor Beare
High Willhays
Gidleigh
Chagford
A382
Blackingstone Rock
Gt. Links Tor
Meldon Hill
B3212
Bridford
Widgery Cross
Hangingstone Hill
Kestor Rock
Moretonhampstead
Christow
Lydford
Brat Tor
W. Okement
Great Kneeset
Cranmere Pool
North Bovey
Easdon Tor
Canonteign Falls
R. Lyd
Fur Tor
N. Teign
Fernworthy Forest
Birch Tor
Grimspound
Manaton
Hayne Down
Bowerman's Nose
Lustleigh
Hennock
Brent Tor
A386
Cut Hill
Bennetts Cross
R. Bovey
Bovey Tracey
R. Tavy
Lynch Tor
Beardown Man
Postbridge
Soussons Down
Hameldown Tor
Jay's Grave
B3193
Mary Tavy
Cowsic
Longaford Tor
Pizwell
E. Webburn
Hound Tor
Holwell Lawn
Peter Tavy
Wistmans Wood
Beardown Tors
Cherry Brook
East Dart
Bellever Tor
W. Webburn
Becka Brook
Haytor
Gt. Mis Tor
Merrivale Quarry
Crockern Tor
Corndon Tor
Widecombe
Saddle Tor
Ilsington
Cox Tor
B3357
Two Bridges
Dunnabridge Pound
Babeny
Rippon Tor
Pork Hill
N. Hessary Tor
West Dart
Swincombe
Dartmeet
Ponsworthy
TAVISTOCK
Whitchurch Common
Vixen Tor
Princetown
Hexworthy
Sharp Tor
Buckland in the Moor
R. Walkham
Black Tor
Whiteworks
Combestone Tor
Bench Tor
Poundsgate
ASHBURTON
B3212
Sharpitor
Foxtor Mires
Childe's Tomb
New Bridge
Horrabridge
Leather Tor
Nun's Cross
Holne
Burrator Reservoir
Sheeps Tor
Ryder's Hill
Buckfast Abbey
Buckland Abbey
Yelverton
Red Lake
Pupers Hill
BUCKFASTLEIGH
R. Meavy
Avon Dam Reservoir
Dewerstone Rock
Cadover Bridge
R. Plym
Erme Plains
R. Avon
Shaugh Prior
China Clay Pits
Stall Moor
Three Barrows
Brent Hill
Lee Moor
Stalldown Barrow
Piles Copse
A385
Cornwood
R. Yealm
R. Erme
Ugborough Beacon
South Brent
Western Beacon
IVYBRIDGE

DARTMOOR

0 1 2 3 4 5 miles
0 1 2 3 4 5 kilometres

D.N.P. Boundary

Landscape above 1500 ft

Woodland

Range Danger Area

SPRING

SPRING MAY COME LATE TO DARTMOOR,
BUT WHEN IT ARRIVES
IT REGISTERS AS A LUMINOSITY
THAT STRENGTHENS
THROUGHOUT THE SEASON.

Previous page: Beardown Man, prehistoric standing stone.

LIGHT AND ROCK

Spring may come late to Dartmoor, but when it arrives it registers as a luminosity that strengthens throughout the season. After months of gloom and violence the first calm day of warmth and light can possess a haunting beauty. Skies are enormous and weather changes are swift and unpredictable. A great landscape has climbed out of winter into the sun and the wilderness has been transfigured into something mysterious and hospitable. Larksong has lost its raw edge and the ache of menace is no longer apparent at dusk. Distances are sketched on haze with hills quivering, more light than land.

Not only does Dartmoor bring us alive in all the senses but it provides an extra spiritual dimension. The sheer physical presence of the wilderness beneath huge skies can swamp the imagination. Walk north on to the open moor beyond Two Bridges and excitement mounts. Then it is possible to share primitive man's instinctive relationship with Nature.

Certainly this is a place of extremes and, when spring's excesses of light wash over the bleakness, the hills seem poised on the frontiers of dream. The tors are remote and unearthly and distances are sunk in silence. Beyond the heat-ripple is the sort of glare which makes the eyes ache. It is difficult to tell where wilderness ends and sky begins or if the whole thing is a mirage.

Love of landscape is inseparable from roots and birthplace; but it is also about folk instinct and a feeling which in the British is very strong. Places, above everything, can conjure up that emotional response. Some of the greatest poems of the nation are really love letters to a particular landscape.

I'm sure there is a state of grace which all creatures discover where the spirit makes its assignation with the seasons. As a boy it occurred for me on the moors. Spring rain and sun had created a dazzling vision. The last shower powdered away, leaving behind it the clarity and stillness of a photograph. The moors smelled as clean as a wild animal, and I was sitting on the most celebrated granite outcrop – Hay Tor –

looking down upon most of South Devon. Far-off farmland was alive with light and beyond the Teign estuary gleamed the Channel. I was peering into an absolute beauty presided over by larksong and the cries of lapwings. Often now, when I have the tor to myself, something remarkable surfaces from childhood.

On the downs, water mirrors the sky and the streams streaking the hillsides are threads of brightness. A shower burnishes the ridge and boggy hollows glitter and the grass moving in the wind carries the shift and stammer of light. This is the world of turf, bracken, hawks and foxes. As cloud shadows glide over the countryside below, sunlight flashes through birds' wings. The wind gusts strong and light swells, fades and swells again. Between the tors are gulfs of sunshine which lift the rocks out of silhouette into hard relief.

Even when the sky is covered with cloud a radiance prevails. Light continues to show in the eyes of animals and in the sheen on the heads of crows and daws.

Going alone to the moors is best, for the spoken word would break the spell. The bones of sheep, the company of gaunt ponies, the curlew calls, the vista and what lies ahead, lost in haze, are enough. They conspire to shape the mystery. A Dartmoor spring brings old realities into focus and the animal experience of walking a ridge without company has its own rewards.

The nuances of weather in bewildering succession change the face of the moors from day to day. I have gone up the Cowsic valley under a navy blue sky lit by lightning. Before noon the storms had rumbled away leaving the heavens cloudless and the smell of rain on drystone walls. The following morning was masked in mist and the cattle on Devil's Tor were standing in a trance. Then sunlight shafted down. The next day was so cold I thought we would get one of those 'blackthorn winters' with enough cuckoo snow to cover the bluebells and primroses of the in-country coombes. The wild daffodils had bloomed at Steps Bridge and I was thinking of them as evening closed.

Again I witnessed the subtle ebb and flow of light in the sky. The moor was darkening, but the dog star firmed to brilliance and the universe arched over me.

**Combestone Tor. Light lifts the rocks out of
silhouette into hard relief.**

Hay Tor from below Saddle Tor.

Southward the hills were blurring on the edge of night and the air was numb with silence. The stars were one of those cosmic dramas which give birth to religions. Prehistoric man must have looked up in awe hoping to find a solution to his human problems among all those small, twinkling lights.

Dartmoor, beneath a night sky full of the optimism of spring, touches spirits blunted by urban life. On the high moor the seasons struggle to win us back. They represent the eternal but the strange granite outcrops on the hilltops are statements of permanence.

There are just under two hundred tors within the three hundred and sixty-five square miles of the National Park. Some are remote, undistinguished and rarely visited; others, notably Hay Tor, provide the unforgettable spectacle of towering grey rock set against the sky. Viewed from the north-west across the Houndtor Valley, Hay Tor has an alpine silhouette on days of bluebell scent and catkin pollen adrift on the breeze.

Tors are scattered all over the moors. Many are obvious landmarks which can be seen for miles. They have a magnetism I can't resist. Walking towards them the old passion for hills beyond hills can carry me for miles at a steady pace. I've never tired of Dartmoor. The smaller, less shapely tors, which don't get in the guide books, have lured me to some fine wilderness country. These little outcrops maintain an exclusive, rather remote air of privacy.

Trips to the north usually end with an ascent of High Willhays. Those well-trodden 2,038 feet of grass and rock make it the highest point on Dartmoor yet it lacks Hay Tor's charisma. The vision of Hay Tor dominates a quarter of Devon. High Willhays is just another lump, however noble, lost among other noble lumps like Rough Tor and Yes Tor. The surrounding hills confine the eye and Okehampton Camp is a grim reminder of the military presence. Civilisation gnaws away at the National Parks and betrayal of wilderness is high on the list of modern transgressions. The vulnerability of such unspoilt countryside makes it the prey of our species' selfishness.

Vixen Tor. An outcrop of many faces.

Over aeons the granite outcrops have been shaved, trimmed and sculpted by the weather – especially frost and ice – but, although many were exposed during the Ice Ages, the moor escaped actual glaciation, hence the broad, shallow valleys and the absence of lakes, ravines, high vertical crags and mountains proper. In his celebrated *Guide to Dartmoor*, William Crossing writes that the tors are the region's most striking features. The gaelic 'torr' means a mound or hill. 'Twr' is Welsh for tower; but the term 'tor' was probably first applied by geologists. Look at Hay Tor, Longaford Tor or Leather Tor and the celtic connection is obvious. They are magnificent granite emminences; but Hay Tor stands supreme. Part of the East Moor's appeal lies in the aesthetic arrangement of Hound Tor, Honeybag Tor, Chinkwell Tor, Rippon Tor, Saddle Tor and Hay Tor, all within short walking distance of each other. They form a natural semi-circle of summits, one leading to the other.

Outcrops, often of startling shape and prominence, cannot fail to catch the eye. They belong to the Age of Fantasy. Among that select band is the lovely Longaford Tor. It rises like a castle at the north end of the broad ridge separating the West Dart from the boggy flats of Powder Mills. I can remember spring nights on its whortleberry and grass terraces, and I have idled away April afternoons up there listening to a cuckoo calling from Wistman's Wood.

Other moorland springs come to mind littered with tors, as if my entire experience of that huge plateau has been a series of journeys from outcrop to outcrop. When I was a boy my first sight of Great Staple Tor printed on mist turned my knees to mush. That love affair with rock and sky and water rendered magical by solitude has never faltered.

I recall a glowing morning on Black Tor above Long-a-Traw water, Hunter's Stone and the hut groups and enclosures before I walked Red Brook Mires to Leftlake Mires and the Stone Row beyond Stalldown Barrow. The South Moor is rich in prehistoric remains and stunning changes of light, and Sharp Tor overlooking Piles Copse provides fine views of the area. Sitting on granite under vast skies in the heat-haze of late spring I've felt the past come alive in a way that prickles the skin.

Merrivale offers Vixen, Staple and Great Mis Tor. 'The Vixen' is an outcrop of many faces, depending on the light, the direction from which it is viewed and the individual imagination. Some see it as a sphinx, others as a fox, while more than a few claim it is the face of a witch. Rising from mist, the tor can seem huge and intimidating but this is an illusion.

Where the in-country begins the copses ring with bird calls, the hedges are choked with flowers and the lanes are full of the stink of wild garlic. The bleak upland silence is only a few stone walls away but beyond the horizon and the tors becalmed in heat-haze are other horizons which can never be reached.

STORIES IN STONE

The rough granite that reaches an art form in many of the tors, pokes out of the landscape almost everywhere. At times it seems to create its own light, especially in the spring when the air becomes visible energy. No wonder the men who worked in stone over the centuries revered it.

Granite responds to the weather and takes on a beauty that is entirely natural. Age helps the process and throughout the wilderness the glory of the rock is celebrated in many forms – weathered crosses, prehistoric remains, drystone walls, houses which refuse to sacrifice their dignity even in dereliction, slabs of moorstone and the tors themselves.

Even the man-made things seem to grow out of the landscape like elements of a timelessness which is the spirit of the place.

Pre-literate man took the granite to build his homes, temples, pounds, stone rows and tombs. From the Neolithic Age into the Bronze Age and beyond, he covered Dartmoor with his work.

At first he used large flat stones collected off the surface of the wilderness. Megalith building flourished for nearly 2,000 years and throughout that period the cromlechs which present no mystery to modern man spread across the moors. Then our ancestors began to set long, narrow stones called menhirs upright in the ground like signposts pointing at heaven.

The enigma of some prehistoric debris continues to produce speculation. Were the stone rows funerary ways, via sacra or ceremonial parades? Were the stone avenues and circles of large stones astronomical 'charts' related to the summer and winter solstices? Were the menhirs reaching for the divine? Were they an awareness of some inextinguishable force made substantial? Life came from the sun and perhaps our ancestors thought the sky could explain the riddle of their own existence with its miseries, joys and fears, and oblivion waiting at the end.

Those pure animal men lived through their instincts and must have been acutely aware of the web of natural forces affecting life. Did they believe the standing stones received power and emanated power? Did they respond to what was for them the inexplicable force that raised flowers and grass in the spring and coaxed leaves out of buds? They must have responded to lightning.

The notion of stones as symbols of a universal awareness and worship of something deathless in Nature and man, should not strike us as far-fetched. We have properties in our bodies which can be found in stones and stars, and knowing water is magnetic to dowsers, can we dismiss any theory which may throw light on that most mysterious age?

Among the less controversial statements in granite to be found on the moors are the shells of Neolithic tombs like Spinsters Rock, and the Bronze Age hut circles of farmsteads and villages such as Grimspound. Many hut circles still show on hillsides, where the remains of field systems and medieaval terraces known as lynchets also endure in ghostly definition. On warm days foxes lie-up in the shallow rings of stone which were once human dwellings and larksong is one of those bridges linking the present with the distant past.

The pounds enclosing some of the settlements were not defensive structures against invading tribes. The one at Grimspound is typical. It contained a Bronze Age village of small huts and all the clan's cattle. The massive drystone walls kept the livestock in and protected them from marauding wolves and bears.

Later in history many pounds were used exclusively to confine farm animals. During the Middle Ages cattle straying onto the Forest of Dartmoor, which was a royal hunting ground, were rounded up and impounded in places like Dunnabridge until their owners were able to pay the fines and obtain their release.

Dunnabridge is first mentioned in 1342 when 'three pence was spent on a new lock for the gate'. In 1732 three hundred and fifty animals were driven there from Erme Pound in a classic moorland drift. Today cultures overlap at Dunnabridge. It stands on the busy Two Bridges–Dartmeet road. Cars speed by as the past

Above top: Spinsters' Rock. The granite remains
of a Neolithic burial chamber.
Bottom: Bronze Age Grimspound with its hut
circles, sheltered in the coombe between Hamel
Down and Hookney Down.
Right: The cross above Horse Ford with distant
Sharp Tor, Hay Tor and Rippon Tor.

re-assembles within the walls. At this time of year the grass is full of the little pink flowers of lousewort and maybe similar flowers decorated corners of the pound when steam rose from the massed cattle as the sun came out after a shower.

Near the entrance is the Judge's Chair or Druid's Chair, as legend will have it, although there were never any druids on the moors. Dubious tradition claims it was scavenged from Crockern Tor where the Stannary Parliament once met. The chair of granite slabs with its granite awning is another impressive piece of stonework.

Although everything on Dartmoor eventually falls apart, like the miles of drystone wall which braid the hillsides and require constant repair, the past is alive with the shadows of things, sounds and disturbing silences. But on Crockern Tor man has left nothing of himself despite the place's connection with a potent period of the moor's history. Today's wilderness is littered with the remains of the tin industry that flourished for centuries. There are old mines, embanked streams, leats and wheel pits, but at Crockern there is only grass, rock and cowpats.

A stannary was a place where tin was mined or worked. The name comes from the late Latin, *stannum*, meaning tin. On Dartmoor there were four Stannary Towns: Plympton, Ashburton, Chagford and Tavistock. They had their own laws, courts and parliament; and the parliament met on Crockern Tor in Lydford Parish. The tor is a short way from the Two Bridges–Postbridge road. It is undistinguished looking.

The Tinners' Parliament was founded over 500 years ago under Royal Charter and for several centuries the ninety-six representatives, twenty-four from each Stannary Town, held infrequent meetings presided over by a warden. The assembly was powerful because the King received a large slice of the industry's profits.

Crockern occupied a position central to the Stannary Towns and overlooked busy mediaeval pack routes. The Tinners' Parliament has slotted comfortably into Dartmoor legend. Seated on stone slabs which formed benches and tables the ninety-six Jurats (or Stannators) passed laws to enforce their rights and privileges. At the Stannary courts rough justice sent offenders and doubtless a few innocents to Lydford and the notorious Stannary gaol.

Village wedding reception for Mary Wedlake at Wonson.

Standing now in the spring sunshine on Crockern Tor, the curlews can be heard crying from Muddilake, and there is no sense of the rock's busy historic past. Walled-in with larksong and sky one can feel utterly alone.

Loneliness can be generated by encounters with the unexpected almost anywhere in the wilderness. A granite cross stepping out of the mist on a spring morning, when even the larks are silent, can make one ache for the company of one's own kind. These crosses were guide posts on remote tracks and old, badly-made roads. Some were boundary markers like Nun's Cross (once called Siward's Cross) which is at least seven hundred and fifty years old.

Loneliness at Grimspound , with its stark hut circles, can be a different sensation altogether. There it strikes as a knowledge of transience and Nature's indifference to human fate.

But with sunshine flying and cloud shadows racing across a windy April afternoon it is difficult to feel anything except elation at the sight of a granite church tower rising above trees and the cawing of rooks.

Right: A March storm over Holne Moor.

Left: Clapper bridge at Postbridge
constructed from slabs of granite. *Above:*
The Dart Valley from Combestone.

Skies are enormous and weather changes are swift and unpredictable.

THE COOMBE

Curlews were calling from their nesting grounds at the top of the coombe. The dawn chorus had ended but birds were still singing in the trees which lined the narrow river where it flowed into the pond, before gushing over a dam to tumble through the wood.

The coombe was broad and long. Eastward were three distinctive tors, a cloudless sky and the sun. To the west was a copse of larch and beech, drystone walls, small fields and a granite farmhouse. Scrub willow and alder grew in the coombe with hawthorn, rowan and birch.

Soon the curlews fell silent but the buzzards which nested in the wood were aloft and loosing their cries. They rode the wind and large eyes decoded the movements in the grass and heather below. Their cat-calls were among the few authentic voices of the wilderness. The big, pale, mottled-brown hawks with their splay-tipped wings descended and the female killed and swung her hooked bill to butcher the rabbit.

The mewling of the raptors was the language of desolation. Presently the birds circled again to read the surface of the coombe. They were only half interested in the nervous flight of lapwings close to the ground near the wellhead of the river.

This part of the coombe was covered in bell heather, ling, bracken, cross-leaved heath and grass, and puddled with black water. Here the lapwings rose and fell on cries which were almost as poignant as the curlew's double-notes. The birds plunged, checked and shot up again with a slipping sideways roll.

Over a hundred springs ago, men quarried granite from the hill on the east side of the coombe and, near the top of a vertical crag, ravens were at their nest. Uttering deep croaks they took wing and, despite their bulk, came down the sky as acrobatically as the lapwings. Calling to each other they dived and rolled and touched bodies three hundred feet above the moor.

It was an astonishing performance - the flying upside down, the sudden plummet, the halt and the gliding, accompanied by soft cries delivered in packages of notes.

Animals love fine weather and the ravens helped the sun's warmth to find its way through their feathers. Dartmoor undulated into the morning and the birds continued to demonstrate their mastery of the east wind. Far below, the frogs on the mire were quiet. Many of them sat motionless in the surface water, amongst cotton grasses, rushes, liverwort, sundews, lichen and mosses.

Beneath them were layers of sphagnum growing on peat gruel. In the water algae registered as a green shine which was as vivid and sinister as the bog moss and brighter than the frogs that were dark, marbled green. Herons often flapped down to swallow frogs before going to the river to fish.

On the edge of the quagmire were bog violets and tormentil, and under the scrub willow, marsh marigolds grew in bushy spreads.

Sunlight flooded the coombe and common lizards emerged to bask on clumps of heather. Adders were already slithering out of the hillside bracken to coil on the bare sheep-walks. With the passing hours the heat stood up and danced. Then over the coombe came the rooks from their nests in the beeches near the farm. Their cawing was an in-country sound for, although the coombe was surrounded on all sides by wilderness, it had a gentle life of its own.

Blackthorn blossom began to rock in the wind that was bending the lady's smocks and wild orchids on the western margins of the river. A curlew called but the buzzards hung silently on their thermal. Half a dozen jackdaws settled in the tops of the willows and the newly minted leaves whitened and blurred back to green again. All along the slopes below the last drystone wall of the farm celandines and wood sorrels were shaking.

The river looped between banks scarred by the hooves of animals and beaded with sheep dung. The water rattled over stones, shillets and pebbles into the shadows under the trees. The heron, that visited the narrow reaches and disturbed the nesting birds with its harsh cry, ate elvers and brown trout which were also taken by mink and the occasional wandering otter.

While the heron stood unmoving at the water's edge, it saw the old dog fox, that

A hard winter followed by a late spring brings
death on Whitchurch Common.

kennelled in the reeds, crossing the bog and lifted with the flap of grey wings. The fox loped stiff-legged over the sphagnum which yielded to his weight. The whole surface quaked and, when a foot broke through a small puddle of peat, ooze was left behind.

Eventually the animal trotted to the river and lapped his own reflection; but for all his alertness he missed the dipper that was walking underwater against the current in search of insects. Avoiding the sunken skull of a pony, the little bird emerged for breath and flew onto a rock and shook itself. Then it uttered two short notes like the clink of metal on metal and dropped into the water again. The fox's eyes narrowed to vertical elipses and he turned and went back to the reed bed.

By noon the wind had risen and the coombe was full of colour in disarray. Thorns ticked and creaked against the drystone walls and grass and reeds were hissing. Higher than the ravens, the buzzards angled their wings and the wind ran off with their cries. The ravens rolled and cronked and dived together before returning to the nest.

The disused quarry was on the edge of the downs and above the upper slopes larks were singing with a passion close to hysteria.

Woken by stems of dead bracken beating against his head and flies clustering the corners of his mouth, the pony foal struggled to stand up. The mare's whinney was answered by other ponies which were searching the hillside for food. On the farmland across the coombe, cattle were belving as they congregated in a field corner out of the wind. Northwards, the heath between two tors was dotted with sheep moving more urgently over the scant grazing.

During the afternoon the wind died. The buzzards had gone but the kestrel falcon was delivering her thin, high-pitched cry as she quartered the flanks of the coombe and fell to squeeze the life out of a vole. The dog fox stirred and raked at his fleas with a rigid hind foot, and the cock wheatear, whose nest of grass and moss was lodged between rocks in the clitter at the foot of the quarry, sang his squeaky song. But nothing could match the shrilling of the larks.

For brief spells the coombe was hushed and the sound of the river was even more pleasant with the trees stilled and the drone and whine of insects rising out of the heat.

Pony herds walked down onto the marshy levels and the mares tugged off mouthfuls of grass. Shadows lengthened and the buzzards returned. Then a JCB opened up on the farmland and a tractor snarled across the pasture above the wood, bringing the lapwings into the air to cry and throw themselves about with neurotic anxiety.

Evening became sunset. Farmwork ceased and the jackdaws gathered noisily on the tors where they nested.

Light faded to dusk and the frogs' chorus spread across the mires. Something large entered the river, a sheep coughed and a dog barked. Vapour lay on the bog and the fox rounded his nostrils to the smells of the coombe as he yawned and stretched. Moths ricochetted off his head when he parted the reeds with his muzzle and analysed the air.

Twilight above the tors was flawless. The hills did not crowd in and suddenly the coombe began to echo with the cries of curlew. The clear sweet double-notes held all the melancholy of wilderness places. Orchestrated by a common desire those pure sounds floated through the stillness. Dozens of birds were in voice and their repeated two syllables carried the landscape into night.

FARMING

The pasture was blotted with daws and rooks and some of the daws stood on the backs of sheep, winkling ticks from the fleeces. The birds were noisy and aggressive and there was a lot of threat display and the flapping of wings.

Beyond the pasture's drystone walls was the broad sweep of the downs with scrub gorse, bracken and heather. The walls were held together by gravity and the skill of the craftsmen that had built them. They separated the common land from the pasture which was a newtake.

The size of a moorland farm was increased by the ancient custom of newtakes. Whenever a new tenant took over one of the ancient tenements he could enclose eight acres of open moor. This right was abolished before the entire place could be walled-in, chiefly by 'improvers' acting illegally.

Between the mid-eighteenth and mid-nineteenth centuries a lot of common land was claimed in this way and the newtakes had been of great importance to farming, at least from the farmer's point of view! The stone walls had protected him from the demands of the commoners. Within the enclosure he was free from discussions about whether or not it was wise to permit grazing. The newtake was his personal bit of the moor. He couldn't run his bull on common land for obvious reasons and because he disliked the thought of the animal serving other people's heifers for nothing.

The home pastures and hayfields north of the down sloped gently to the farmhouse of grey stone at the top of the in-country cleave. Southward the landscape bulged, flattened and ended abruptly in sky. Cattle were jostling each other in the yard, and calves and heifers occupied the pen against the side of the milking shed, which was a byre with a hayloft and granite walls. The sharp sting of ammonia from soiled bedding was on the air and liquid manure splattered onto the cobbles. Around the rooftops house martins flickered and the hum of insects could be heard whenever the animals stopped bawling.

Owen and Joe White at Batworthy Farm.

Beryl Hutchings of Dury Farm, Bellever.

Farming continues as the most important influence on the moors. Not only do the animals bring the landscape to life but they keep it open by the simple process of grazing. There are few places elsewhere in Britain where ponies, sheep and cattle may be seen sharing the same stretch of hills.

Dartmoor's agriculture is determined by the weather, the terrain and the soil. Its pastoral origins reach back to Neolithic times. Toughness is the key to the entire business and today's Galloway cattle are as hardy as the Scottish Blackface sheep which now roam the exposed upland with the ponies all year round.

But a late spring following a severe winter claims victims even among animals bred to endure some of the worst weather Britain can brew. Sheep carcasses on bare hillsides and dead or dying pony mares and foals suggest something is very wrong with the present farming policy. During the bleakest months in the bleakest areas competition for food is intense. Then there is no food and the weakest creatures perish, miserably. Spring's most awful irony is the pitiful spectre of neglect – skeletal mares, too far gone to eat; dying foals trying to suckle dead mothers.

On the high moor there are commons. Common grazing was enjoyed by the venville or in-country farms and the true moor properties. Along the edge of Dartmoor, green cultivated land meets heath and mire with a dovetailing of enclosed fields and wilderness. It is the frontier of in-country that is composed of border farms and small communities.

As always on Dartmoor the past and granite are hard to escape. Roughly a hundred and fifty years after the Norman Conquest stone buildings began to replace the wooden farmhouses. Some were of great length and over the centuries were modified and altered by generations of yeoman farmers. The present examples of these longhouses are beautiful. They are as solid as tors and were built to take whatever a hill country winter could throw at them.

Here people and animals lived under the same thatched roof – cows and calves in the shippen and just across the dividing passage the family in the kitchen.

The idyllic co-existence of people and livestock continued until the 1920s when hygiene laws exiled the animals to separate cowsheds; but even today there are still longhouses with beasts in the shippen end.

Longhouses were central to the holdings known as ancient tenements, some of which still survive as working farms. The thirty-five ancient tenements were situated along the lower valleys of the West and East Dart rivers, and the Wallabrook valley within the Forest of Dartmoor. Their occupants held them by copyhold, which indicates their early date, since copyhold could only be established if occupancy was already 'time out of mind' or, in other words, customary. The tenements which live on with their lovely old field systems, architecture and driftways are a testament to the animal husbandry of yesterday enshrined in the unity of man and Nature.

The commons remain integral to modern agriculture and not so long ago Down-Country farmers sent their stock to summer on the high moors. The cattle were driven by dogs and mounted stockmen in great drifts up the in-country lanes onto the moor, where they were split into small herds and taken to different parts of the grazing.

The commons are held by various landowners subject to the rights of others. These common rights are in the deeds of moorland properties. The 1985 Dartmoor Commoners' Act led to the formation of the Devon County Council Dartmoor Commoners' Association which regulates the use of the land in question. The idea was to prevent overgrazing and overstocking. At last animal welfare headed a list of priorities, but sheep and ponies continue to die in wretched circumstances whenever man opts out of his stewardship.

Our forefathers respected the environment and what it harboured. They took from nature and gave back to nature, for they understood the primary laws governing man's partnership with the planet.

What they built in stone survives but their way of life and simple philosophy have been forgotten or rejected. Yet the work with sheep continues to bring the past alive.

Leaving the stand of oaks where wood anemones were dancing in the wind beneath the trees, the farmer rode his horse slowly out of the coombe, followed by a couple of border collies. A hard, stinging shower hammered down and the cuckoo pints in the hedge were soon full of water. Behind the early morning rain came the sun and presently the hillside was glistening. Horse and rider climbed the hill onto the down and the sheep began to run. The Scottish Blackfaces were wiry, alert creatures, slight of build and heavy fleeced. Several of their kind elsewhere on the high moor had carried lambs for over five months only to die of exhaustion and starvation while in labour. The farmer had come to 'look over' his animals. The ewes ran before him, calling to their lambs and lifting masks of timid enquiry.

The lean, black and white dogs were intelligent. Without them moorland sheep farming would be impossible. Early in their training the farmer had recognised placid dispositions which pedigree alone could not guarantee. He had mastered the dogs and educated them in sheep lore. Now they had the demeanor of champions and never barked and rarely hurried.

Another shower fell and afterwards the moors were filmed with light. The sheep continued to scatter but the Galloways stood and watched the horseman approach. The shower drifted on over North Bovey and Moretonhampstead. In one of the fields of Shilstone Farm near Drewsteignton, the granite of Spinsters' Rock was darkening in the fade-away of the sun. When the rain fell the jack hare dozing within the cromlech half opened his eyes and stretched his forelegs. Raindrops pattered on the capstone but the hare was asleep before the sun shone again.

THE TEN TORS – 1985

Saturday May 17th: I drove through the darkness to meet the rain the other side of Yelverton. The day was only a few hours old but already it looked grim.

In the grey first light the tent city in front of Okehampton Camp was wet and dreary, despite the orange canvas flapping in the gale. By now the rain was torrential and teenagers in cagoules and walking boots were scurrying about trying to postpone the inevitable drenching.

The military policeman glanced at my pass and waved me through the gates onto roads crowded with small figures shouldering enormous back-packs. It was a quarter of an hour to the start of the annual Ten Tors event which is divided into three distances: thirty-five, forty-five and fifty-five miles, each of which offered four different routes. Soon three hundred and ninety-three teams of youngsters would squelch off over the moors, despite the atrocious weather that had created the worst conditions in the twenty-seven year history of the event.

The 2,358 boys and girls were expected to be well-clad and well-trained, and the back-up of helicopters, military personnel and vehicles, the St. John Ambulance and the Dartmoor Rescue Groups was confident it could cope with any emergency.

Rain deluged the hill where the walkers were massing and I saw one boy in football shorts and several young people without waterproof cagoules.

'They've been told and checked and they've chosen the hard way,' said the experienced mountaineer beside me. Despite their training, they were definitely not giving Dartmoor the respect it deserved on such a cold, wet and windy day.

The padre said a short prayer then, as the kilted piper began to play *Amazing Grace*, the teams stampeded down the hillside towards the television cameras. Half a dozen youngsters immediately sprawled full-length in the Moor-Brook but their enthusiasm could not be denied.

Watching them disperse and head in their groups of six towards Rough Tor, West

Mill Tor or Yes Tor I remembered walking this country when I was a teenager and I knew how they were feeling. To be young and fit is glorious, and The Ten Tors allows participants to test themselves in wild country on Nature's terms.

Thirty odd years ago I came to these hills with a hunger for what they offered. Even then I never thought of myself as a stranger among the granite outcrops. The spirit of adventure is passed from generation to generation, and always it is carried forward by the young.

A little later I walked up the loop road to watch the beginning of the special event for the physically and mentally handicapped. Over a hundred and fifty gathered in the dark haze of rain, some in wheelchairs, accompanied by a friend or relative, others shadowed by young soldiers. It was profoundly moving. Only thirteen were to drop out.

I spent the rest of the morning in the camp speaking to helicopter crews, soldiers, the event controller and various media people. But I was back on the loop road after lunch to see the participants in the special event arriving at the finish. Seven miles in a wheelchair, along a route 1,200 feet above sea level, on one of the wettest and most depressing spring days I can recall, is a real achievement. What yardstick can be used to measure such stoicism and willpower? I promised myself from then on that, when I was tempted to carp about my lot, I would summon up the vision of a young girl working her wheelchair out of the rain gloom, soaked to the skin but undismayed.

Throughout the day The Ten Tors dominated radio and television news. The swollen rivers, the mires and surface water, the bitter east winds gusting to force nine and ten, and the rain all took their toll of the walkers. The rescue groups were kept busy bringing in cases of mild hypothermia, and many wet and cold youngsters could not face the prospect of a night under canvas in what must have seemed a very hostile environment after dark.

Sunday May 18th: By morning the 'drop-out' list was growing rapidly, and arriving at the camp I saw a Wessex helicopter land close to the administration tent. Out came the rucksacks, then a couple of girls wrapped in blankets were helped towards the waiting military ambulance. Around three hundred and fifty exhausted teenagers, aged between fourteen and nineteen, were already bedded down in one of the halls, and others had been assisted back to their base camp.

The rain had stopped but the wind was still cold. A journalist said he thought the event should have been cancelled but I don't think he understood the situation. How do you tell nearly two and a half thousand young people, most of whom have thoroughly prepared for The Ten Tors, that the whole thing is off – at the last minute?

Some walkers made their own way back to base with the route unfinished. There was talk of streams in flood which had to be waded waist-deep; of wet gear and wet clothes, and mental and physical fatigue. All morning the helicopters came and went, and it was evident that less than four hundred participants would complete the event within the allotted time of two days.

Among the drop-outs was the boy in the black football shorts. It was no surprise, but the rebel in me had wished him luck.

Towards noon a group was seen approaching the camp. It proved to be the scouts of Torquay Boys Grammar School – the 20th Torbay: four fifteen-year-olds and two fourteen-year-olds. They were the first home in the thirty-five mile section, but in The Ten Tors there are no winners or losers, for the youngsters are not competing against Nature or other teams. Man doesn't conquer mountains. He walks on them and climbs them but the hills remain unmoved by his problems and celebrations.

Yet crossing high, wild country in less than ideal conditions we may learn something about ourselves. For many the actual taking part in an event like this is enough. For others it will be the beginning of a lifetime love affair with the hills, rooted in quiet self-confidence.

Ultimately, perhaps, the conservation of British wilderness will depend on those who love and understand it and can argue on its behalf from the strength of a hard won affinity.

Floodwater on the North Moor with Yes Tor and High Willhays.

MORAL HORIZONS

One morning I had had enough of desolation and left the North Moor to come to Manaton Rocks above the village of that name. Situated among scrub oak, rowan and holly, the outcrops provide splendid views of the in-country with glimpses of nearby wilderness. The Rocks crown a low hill covered in walled fields. Beneath the trees the bluebells were the kind of deep colour that surprises the eye and the oak leaves were more gold than green. A blackbird sang, the sun shone and scent was rising from the flowers.

I sat on the turf with my back to the granite and listened to the keening of buzzards, a sound that is rarely absent from this part of Devon. Beside me was a scattering of rabbit droppings dried to fibrous buckshot by the sun. Then I saw the adder. It had dragged its slackness out of the bracken by the trees to sunbathe on one of the small rocks a few feet below me. I love this snake and have never subscribed to the mythology which has given it a bad reputation. There are many adders on Dartmoor and I see them every spring and summer. Heathland everywhere provides sanctuaries for a declining population as habitat continues to shrink.

The snake's tongue flickered to collect scent particles and present them to the sense organ in the roof of its mouth. The flickering detected smells. The creature was deaf but sounds registered as vibrations through the skull. When I walked the pony paths I always brought down my boots heavily to warn the snakes I was coming.

Sharing the morning of birdsong and warmth with the creature was satisfactory. Yet all over the country it is persecuted out of ignorance and fear. Once during a boyhood trip to Dartmoor I heard an old woman say as she stood over the body of an adder killed by her son: 'Why did God make un?' She was asking the mindless question which typifies human reaction to the rest of creation: 'Why does anything exist if we don't have a use for it?'

A creature is rarely weighed for its own worth and often we find it difficult to think of a wilderness like Dartmoor without subjecting it to our values.

Mass activities are acceptable if they are once-a-year happenings like The Ten Tors; but when a kind of cult fever takes over, the consequences must cause unease in those who care.

Gregariousness on a place like Dartmoor is difficult to understand if you are by nature a loner. These days there are more people walking the National Park in groups, large and small, than at any other time in its history. Letter-boxing is contributing to the overcrowding as the hobby grows in popularity.

The first letterbox was put on the moor at Cranmere Pool in the mid-nineteenth century by Mr Perrot of Chagford. From a tin where friends could leave their visiting cards the innocent pastime has mushroomed into the situation we have today with groups tramping all over the National Park in search of more and more boxes. The thirty of ten years ago have become the two thousand-plus of today. The number of people out searching for letterboxes every weekend can't be good for the wilderness. I remember meeting upwards of twenty poking about on Cox Tor one Sunday morning for the elusive Kestrel Box.

The old idea of a small number of boxes where you could leave your postcard with your name, address and a stamp on it for the next walker who came along to collect and put in a real postbox in his home town sounds fine. It must have been interesting to see where it came from. Now the rubber stamp in the box is the big attraction and 'Boxers' have their little books in which they collect them. Some of the so-called 'letterboxes' are plastic ice-cream containers and supermarket shopping bags.

It's the vogue among the dedicated to create new boxes and one cannot help thinking the actual collecting side of the hobby is more important for some than walking the moor between each site. Personally I 'collect' tors simply because so many of them occupy superb stretches of wilderness or are tucked away in secret corners.

Wherever large groups of people regularly walk, the open moor must suffer. If letterboxing gets out of hand it could pose problems for the National Park Authority

Arthur Brown putting the geese to bed, Moor Gate.

which has a responsibility not only to the place but also to human recreational needs. Maybe two thousand letterboxes are almost two thousand too many.

If you prefer the company of one or two friends, or are content to go alone, the erosion of solitude by mass activity will grate. Yet there are so many ways in which an area as vulnerable as Dartmoor can be diminished – too much noise, too many people moving about together, too many self-serving commercial enterprises whose impact on the landscape or animal life is insidious or dramatically obvious. Silt from forestry operations gets into the upper reaches of rivers and covers the salmon spawning beds.

A vet's bill could wipe out the profit on the sale of a pony, so some sick animals are left to suffer and die. These are facets of diminishment.

The broad moral horizons beyond species selfishness remain distant, but we have to strive for them or we are lost and Dartmoor is lost. The longhouses appear to grow out of the landscape. What a pity Big Business agriculture, like the Duchy of Cornwall's, has decided to invest in Big Business development. The new giant barns are alien structures standing like threats on the skyline. This is architecture debased to a physical blow. The sight of it halts you in your tracks.

The great country writer Richard Jefferies said: 'Where man goes, nature ends.' In the past farming enriched the Dartmoor landscape and gave it much of the character we have come to love. It was a man-sized concern, but now it is machine-sized, opening up a new profit-making dimension which has proved as destructive in the wrong hands as it is selfish and unpleasant.

Machinery grinding away at this place could undo the work of centuries in an afternoon; but there's some light at the end of the tunnel, for the farmer may now get a grant to repair drystone walls! Yet the economics are still wrong. Healthy country-side and wilderness are needed more than butter mountains, grain and beef mountains and wine lakes.

In the end there is a conflict of priorities. Do we conserve or exploit? The moor isn't a museum but there are a growing number of people who love it and wish to protect it from powerful concerns. Human interests should exist organically within the limitations of the National Park or twenty centuries of growth in a state of history will accelerate into a swift retreat from the wisdom of the past.

Greed appears to be a perennial factor in man's dealings with the moor. Landowners 'improve' farming facilities by putting up the huge new barns. Then up go the rents, putting pressure on the tenant to get as much as possible out of his land. It would be tragic if 'Where man goes, Nature ends' became prophetic in Dartmoor's case.

SUMMER

ON A SUMMER DAY THE STREAM IS
ALIVE WITH ITS OWN LIGHT
AND BROWN TROUT RING THE SURFACE
ALL ALONG THE FLAT REACHES.

Previous page: Bill Haydon's reed comber, Whiddon Down.

CONTRASTS

The wind was whispering and sending light and dark green waves across the great blanket bog where the grass was deep enough to hide a standing fox. The hills on three sides were crowned with tors and the grass was flowing endlessly towards them.

Down in the reedy depression, which was the source of the river, there was more evidence of the brief plenitude that visits the wilderness in summer. Among patches of sphagnum were the small white flowers of sundews and white-tufted cotton grass. Winged insets droned among the peat hags, pools of bog water and the lichens, liverworts and mosses of the North Moor.

The greens of the blanket bog were vibrant and intense. Again the shimmer passed across the mire and the whispering was carried to the hills and the sky, with its clouds massing to form those impossible horizons which haunt every season on Dartmoor. Acres of solitude lay open to larksong and the croaking of ravens. With the weather fair and greenness pulsing and quaking under the wind the animals running free were content.

The early morning gathering of ponies at the roadsides in tamer places was underway. The animals are the small, tough descendants of the celtic ferals which probably grazed the wastes before the Romans came. Over generations their whole character and physique has been shaped by man to suit his purpose. They have always fed themselves, roaming a wide area but now they have become a mixed bunch and very few pure-bred Dartmoors are to be seen.

The nineteenth century produced a boom in ponies. They were wanted for the coal mines, carts and traps and as pets children could ride. The introduction of Shetland pony stallions at this time created small hardy animals suitable for the mines. Those days have gone but in modern times the freedom of the hills can be a death sentence imposed by over-stocking.

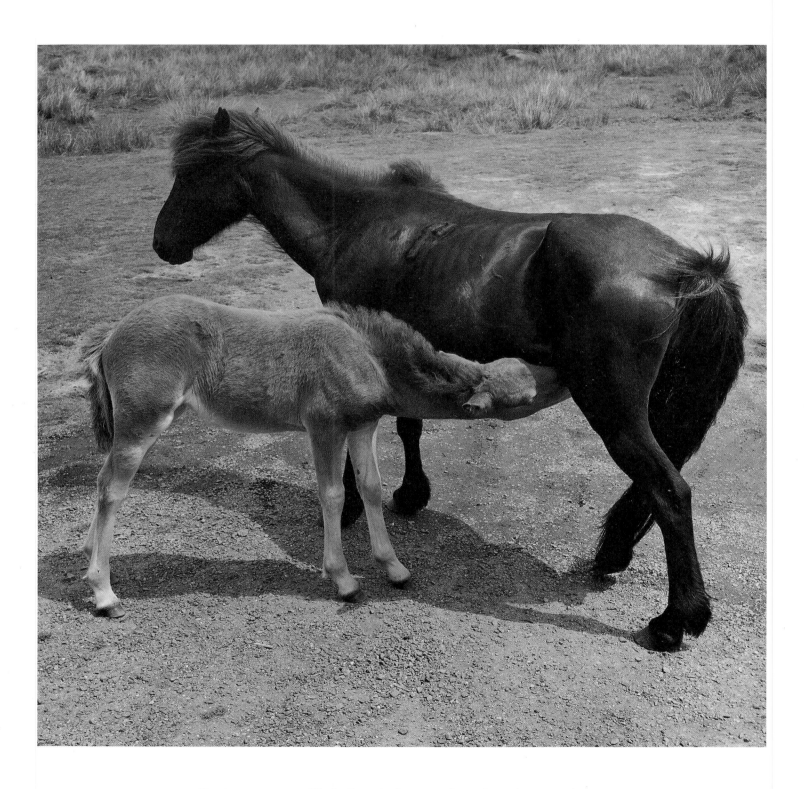

Dartmoor mare and foal – farmstock, an unplanned tourist attraction.

Ponies are farm animals and elements of a casual unplanned tourist attraction, featuring on the National Park's symbol.

The brood mares and their foals paced to the roadside and waited while down on the A38 dual carriageway the holiday traffic was building up. Dust haze and petrol fumes released cars and caravans and coaches. They came unsteadily out of the heat to follow the tourist trails onto the moors, where the air was stirring visibly like the draught from a hot oven.

The ponies were patient. They arched their necks and snuffled or contorted their bodies to scratch in characteristic postures. Foals gazed about, unable to come to terms with the small incidents which blitzed their knowing: a bee thudding gently against a muzzle; the musk of gorse; ceaseless larksong; the whack and rush of wings as daws passed overhead; the cries of sheep; the roar of a milk tanker grinding through the gears as it struggled uphill.

Then the cars appeared and slowed down at the sight of the animals. Ponies were Dartmoor, place made flesh and blood. Strategically placed along the road are signs warning visitors that the feeding of the animals is forbidden by law; but the fifty pound maximum fine did not deter the young couple with their toddler.

The van pulled in, and an arm pushed through the open side-window. One of the mares walked boldly up to the hand offering the iced bun and began to eat. An instamatic clicked, the woman laughed and the baby chuckled. Then the family got out and the man with great stupidity put the child on the mare's back and another photograph was taken of baby's first horseride, which could have ended in tragedy. The rest of the herd gathered round.

Another car drew to a halt and a helicopter sailed overhead. Looking down some moments later the pilot was already over the wilderness. For six miles or so he followed the course of the East Dart until it became lost in the wind patterns of the grass of the great mire.

WATER

Near Cranmere Pool on the North Moor, five rivers are born: the Tavy, Teign, Taw, Okement and East Dart. They emerge from the blanket bog as trickles which become streams that race downwards to pick up the status of rivers on their way to the sea. It is difficult to resist the movement and sound of running water or the way it holds the light of the sky and juggles with it. Most people have streams of childhood, full of trout and happy memories.

Why is water so fascinating? Do we regard it as the birthplace of humanity, our original element? Can race instinct reach back that far in time? Dartmoor streams, like most upland torrents, are bold gestures, capable of the unexpected flash flood, but usually they are harmless narrows, gushing among jumbles of rocks until they glide through the lowland woods and fields to their estuaries. Whenever I'm absent from Devon and get homesick for the moors, I see the Becka Brook and my heart is heading for home long before I start the car.

The Becka Brook bursts from the ground on the East Moor at Seven Lords Lands to divide Houndtor Valley and run through Houndtor Woods into the River Bovey. On a summer day the stream is alive with its own light and brown trout ring the surface all along the flat reaches. Dark fish ghost over the grit into pools the colour of barley wine, cider or milkless tea, depending on how much sun they hold. Below the bridge of granite, the trout swims swell after a night's rain and the spate carries froth down from the shallows. Sunshine glints on pebbles, gravel and stones where the movement of fish is swift and exciting. The stream spills between mossy rocks and humps of storm debris and fizzes like lemonade full of small shadows which glide into deeper shadow and hang there with hardly a twitch of the tail.

The brown trout are surface feeding, nosing into the current. Every now and then a fish slaps the surface and sinks again to skim along the grit under slack water. Then there is a glimpse of red spots on dark glossy brown with a hint of gold.

Sometimes the water washes over pebble-littered shallows, swilling around islands of silt and branches created by spring floods until it empties into silence. Here the mayflies dance and trout surface to feast on the drift of insects. All the calm places are patrolled by fish that snap up caddis, stoneflies, water fleas, mays and beetles. Water forget-me-nots, rushes and sedges choke the margins, and water crow-foot provides cover for the minnows. Only the dragonflies whizzing and clicking over the surface manage to avoid the snapping jaws.

In the upland woods, the stream is narrower and fiercer, but, wherever it broadens, there is the flurry and flicker of trout. They weave their dizzy patterns or cruise among the jumbles of rocks. Alders, beeches, hazel, oak and ash make arches of foliage over the water. Woodpigeons croon but the summer day is honeycombed with the muted roar and splash of the Becka Brook as it flows over boulders into pools. The mayflies which spent three years underwater as larvae are also on the wing, but having no mouths they starve to death after a few hours if they escape being eaten.

House martins and swallows scoop the insects off the surface with a barely audible clack of closing beaks. They come low across the meadow in front of Leighon House, diving, twisting and screaming. The smell of green plants fills the morning and the mewling of buzzards cuts across the drowsy tinkle of the water.

The upper reaches are swift and florescent but before it enters the wood the Becka Brook pours into Leighon Pond. Here the dizzy swirl settles to flat calm. Many creatures use this secluded spot. Canada geese nest on the little island, although a complete brood of young birds rarely survives due to the mink. Water voles, foxes, herons, mallard, moorfowl, daws, crows, rooks, stoats and numerous songbirds all come to the Pond. Trout leap and flop back, making the cattle in the field beyond the rowans and hawthorns prick their ears.

Every corner of the moors has a stream or river of individual character. The Upper Cowsic flows through a deep valley of bracken and grass beneath Devil's Tor and the celebrated standing stone, Beardown Man which is nearly eleven feet high. There are few birds to bring the landscape out of its stillness. Occasionally ravens fly

The Tavy, as it runs through the Cleave, can fill a grey summer morning after rain with noise and brightness.

over the hills but the head waters of this river, like so many others, course through vast solitudes. Yet a stream in a lonely place can warm the heart and the Tavy in spate, churning through the Cleave, is a sight few spirits would not rise to. It can fill a grey summer morning after rain with noise and brightness.

Walking the mires west of the Cowsic, you cross the West Dart and descend Broad Down to the East Dart and the waterfall below Sandy Hole Pass. It is a good stretch of moor with the heather yet to bloom and bracken stirring in the wind.

The Dart is my favourite river. Whenever I see it behind my thoughts there is the flash of sunlight through rowan leaves and the stony scent of water and moss. Going alone up the East Dart to Cranmere I am confronted by the familiar invested with a splendour springing directly from the whole wilderness experience. Many find bleakness and solitude intolerable; but what can seem a hostile environment to the casual visitor may be an area of immense interest to those who love it for what it is.

Perhaps the average person feels interrogated by solitude and shrinks from its implications. But if we decide to go to wilderness Dartmoor we should meet it on Nature's terms. What can we give of ourselves to the place? We cannot increase the beauty of the high moor. Caring deeply for a landscape does not sweeten the larksong or make the grass radiant. But we can tarnish that beauty or destroy it out of stupidity, avarice or carelessness. By remaining faithful to Nature we remain faithful to our better selves.

There is a dangerous arrogance in the assumption that everything in the world has been laid out for our benefit. It is a pity Dartmoor is known as a 'National Park'. Park has all the implications of order, neatness and discipline. The municipal park syndrome is that compulsive desire to tidy-up nature and reduce it to the level of lawns, herbaceous borders and flowerbeds. In a world of vanishing wilderness to tame the high moor would be a crime.

Yet I am arguing from a human need – the need for the sort of solitude and serenity Dartmoor has in abundance. The River Dart caters for everyone – loners and crowd lovers. Its upper reaches attract the few and the tourist 'honey pots', from

Postbridge down, provide for the many. From places like Postbridge, Dartmeet and Buckfast Abbey, the Dart can be viewed without straying far from the car. The 'beauty spots' offer Nature on solid human terms and attract crowds of people at the busiest time of year. Although the actual places have been turned into little urban oases, it isn't difficult to imagine how wild and lovely they must have been before they became popular. But it is so natural for everyone to be fascinated by water and the beauty spots and other tourist centres are the salvation of the high moor.

The long days among the hills and green coombes unfold as the season brings a gentleness to the granite upland. Sheep and lambs stray across the down and become part of the slow parade of cloud shadow. Rain falls and lifts scent off the mires. Bleating mingles with larksong and the sound of running water. A herd of ponies shatters the sun-dazzle on the stream. Cattle roll in peat wallows as the flies zoom in to greedy on lips and eyes. A cow suckles three young pigs in a farmyard. The roadside pony mares and foals continue to beguile and scrounge; the foolish stop and feed them, unaware that they are encouraging the animals to court death. At night a pony is difficult to see and runs the risk of being knocked down and killed or badly injured. Others fall victim to the 'cowboy' driver gunning his car along at lunatic speeds as if Dartmoor's roads are part of some on-going rally.

But death in the middle of so much life suits the crows picking over the bones of something that was once a fox. The crows often nest in small hawthorn trees and go about the business of eating carrion. The yellow flowers of bog asphodel stand motionless while the birds examine their find. Some people believe crows are evil. They are not. They are just crows and, like the other creatures enjoying the summer, they live through each moment as it comes.

THE TOURIST MOOR

There is a curiosity in many people that takes them to the top of somewhere to look back towards the place they have just left. Residents from all around the moor – Plymouth, Exeter, Okehampton, Torbay – are pulled to familiar high ground on fine weekends to sit in the sun and gaze over their 'home territory'. The mysterious appeal of distance viewed from the sky liberates us from that earth-bound feeling which attends much of daily life.

A warm Sunday afternoon will bring the crowds to Pork Hill car park on the west side of the moor and to Hay Tor which dominates the east. On a clear day the views from Pork Hill present immense vistas of the West Country looking beyond the Tamar to Cornwall and Bodmin Moor. Hay Tor car park lies on the opposite edge of the plateau, where the moor plunges dramatically to the in-country and the eye is carried across the small hills of South Devon to the English Channel. Berry Head light flashing through a summer dusk, with distances blueing and the glow of Torbay's street lamps beginning to show, can make the heart swell.

The Sunday gathering-places, where the Devon accent is heard, gives locals and visitors the chance to relax and reflect and soak up the beauty. For a lot of people that's enough. They may be aware of the wilderness beyond Cox Tor and Great Staple Tor but they like to sit and face a gentler landscape. The majority love Dartmoor and being up there in the sun close to the tors and ponies is enough. The car parks, with their buzzard's eye view of Devon and opportunities to walk in safety, are ideal for the casual visitor, the elderly or families with very young children.

For the tourist, Dartmoor is many things: Baskerville country, a big high misty place of weird rocks, heather, ponies, rivers, Widecombe and Princetown's notorious prison. The three P's of Tourism remain significant: Prison, Ponies and Pixies. The fourth, perhaps, is P for People in pursuit of other people! The holiday highways run from one spot to another like a pilgrimage route to Mammon's shrines: Widecombe,

Right: Layers of Dartmoor.
Chagford Common dissects Fernworthy Forest and farmland.
Above: Annie Monro's pigs supplement their diet at Smith Hill Farm.

Left: Bennett's Cross,
with heather-clad mine workings, and Birch Tor.
Above: Down Tor stone row on Hingston Hill.

The menhir at Merrivale.

Postbridge, Lydford Gorge, Becky Falls, Dartmeet, Buckfast Abbey, Princetown. Fortunately for the area visitors always want to spend money, as if putting one's hand in one's pocket is part of the ritual of having a good time. But what Princetown has to offer is free.

Dartmoor Prison, seen from the roadside through summer drizzle, is grim with all the greyness of the dark moorland rock. Its history goes back nearly two hundred years, when England and France were at war and French prisoners were crammed into hulks off Plymouth. Soon there were thousands of men living in miserable circumstances; but every age has its great opportunists and the early years of the nineteenth century produced an inspired entrepreneur, Sir Thomas Tyrwhitt, Lord of the Stannaries. He decided to 'develop' the wilderness east of North Hessary Tor, so he built a village called Prince's Town (named after his patron, the Prince Regent). Reclaiming the moor for farmland would require a large labour force and, as the French prisoners were doing nothing useful, Sir Thomas thought it would be a good idea to create a war prison as part of the village and put the inmates to work.

During their incarceration many prisoners died from illness, starvation, general hardship and even duelling! Late in the prolonged hostilities with France the French at Princetown were joined by some of their American allies. It was a typical P.O.W. 'camp' with the inmates administering their own affairs from within and the guards on the perimeter platform making sure they didn't escape. The circular construction of the prison gave the guards a clear and comprehensive range of musket fire, but anyone who made it over the wall found the open moor waiting like a predator. Generally discipline prevailed with senior officers in control under the prison governer. But existence was hazardous and fifteen hundred French and two hundred and eighteen Americans perished. At the end of hostilities, the surviving prisoners were repatriated and the prison became a small industrial area for a while before it was closed.

It was reopened as a convict prison in 1852. When Captain Stockford became the governor in 1860, he was shocked to see the whitening bones of the French and

American dead poking from the ground where they had been buried. He had the remains laid to rest properly in the French and American cemeteries with separate obelisks as marks of respect. These cemeteries are there today, on prison property, and the stained-glass window installed in Widecombe Church by the American Daughters of the Revolution in 1910 is a poignant reminder of hard times.

Princetown hasn't lost any of its harshness. For most of the year it is a cold, wet place and even a summer day has a touch of granite in its austerity; yet the cars still pull up in the layby and the occupants get out to peer over the fields at the prison sprawl. Binoculars are raised and the windows scanned in the hope of glimpsing a waving figure. But inside there is hardly a view of the moor. The work parties, marching out of the gates to the now successful farm, have enough desolation at close hand each day without trying to re-acquaint themselves with it from a cell window set beyond their reach. The 'beauty' of the moor has little value for men longing for home.

There is something unpleasant about the people who come to gloat. The fortunates gaze into the living nightmare of fellow human beings from the privileged side of the walls as if the prisoners' deprivations, however well-deserved they may be, spice the onlooker's enjoyment of personal liberty which is beyond value.

The ponies plodding along the grass verges are a diversion from 'jailbird-watching'. Cuddly animals in a picturesque setting are always welcome as the great emptiness of Dartmoor breeds its mild anxieties. The pony has stepped out of the green sign which lets you know you are in the National Park and animals trailing across a busy road will start the cameras clicking and raise a chorus of 'oohs' and 'ahs'. Fingers squeak on charabanc windows to rub off the mist and children plead to take the little ones home. Then the coaches roll on down the hill into Widecombe where ponies are rarely absent from the green. Here they thread through the crowds and the traffic while pub-grub and cream teas find their way into folk who are enjoying themselves. Once in a while, though, someone irritates a mare and gets kicked. Pixies are easier to handle.

Nell White's mantelshelf, Lower Meripit, Postbridge.

The boom in garden gnomes and pixies is the pleasantly daft side of the tourist trade, but there are those who insist the moor is the home of a secretive tribe of midgets. These rosy-cheeked dandiprats sport pointed hats and green hose and carry a lot of loose flesh. Replicas of them stand with their painted grins outside shops and cafés. Pixies or puckies or piskies feature in Dartmoor legend but never as the colourful toys on sale, which get life sentences in surburban gardens.

Maybe giving pixies the status of real creatures is a recognition of the need for a magical extension to human existence beyond the limitations of science, reason and logic. But the nice garden pixies aren't like the dwarves which scuttled about in the margins of my childhood. They were wicked, potato-nosed, warty little devils capable of compromising the tom cat after four pints of scrumpy. The bright red and green figures sell and find their way all over Britain; and looking out across the lawn at one, somebody somewhere may relive an afternoon of strawberries and cream in a Dartmoor village.

The café is central to the tourist moor. Coaches don't just head for the tors and rivers and ponies. They roar towards the cream tea – the buttered scones, clotted cream and jam, served al fresco or in cool cafés away from the wasps and heat. Cream teas and dairy fudge are to Devon what tartan and haggis are to Scotland. And why not? An afternoon on Hamel Down leaves one hungry and thirsty. Then a pot of tea and scones and cream is a feast. And so is a hot dog in Hay Tor car park with the memory of a long wet walk heavy in one's legs.

Alan's refreshment van with its ice creams, lollies, hot dogs, cold drinks and tea is as important to the tourists as the tor itself. The car is parked and in five minutes the entire family can be standing on the summit of this most famous rock – 1,490 feet above the sea. During the school holidays it is often covered with children. Coaches arrive at the car park, the occupants scramble out and race up to the tor, laughing and joking, then they return happy, to polish off ice creams and depart – for Widecombe. The Dartmoor car park is a microcosm of the urban situation set down in the wilderness.

Pork Hill, Hay Tor and Dartmeet are examples of them as playgrounds as well as areas where the car (the little home on wheels) stands ready for the return to the familiar. The Devon seaside has been invaded by folk from the north and midlands so the comparatively uncluttered moor becomes the native's sanctuary and two thirds of the people using it live in Devon.

Ponies visit almost every car park on the moor and the views or the surroundings are usually enough to satisfy most tastes in the outdoors. The change of environment is sufficient and the actual ugliness of Dartmeet with its misnamed Badger's Holt Café passes unnoticed except perhaps by wilderness eccentrics! In such places people exercise dogs, amble about or chat or doze. At Postbridge they spend a few moments looking at the Clapperbridge, have lunch in the pub and sit by the river or return to their cars. Then the chaffinches descend and make a noise until they are fed and the ponies approach with rolling haunches and liquid brown eyes, like the stars of the whole Dartmoor show. No beauty spot is complete without them.

On a busy Sunday at the height of the holiday season Dartmeet is a huge noisy housing estate of cars, but the people stuck there enjoy it all. They are on the threshold of a beauty which eclipses for a few hours the sameness of existence. There is the need for change and escape, not alone but as a loose community. Perhaps the most unacceptable thing in urban life is uncertainty and the tourist honey pots acknowledge this.

OTHER PLACES

Roadside tourism is good for the open moor with its wildlife and plant life. All most visitors ask for is a sunny day, plenty to see and somewhere to aim at.

One of the less-crowded targets is Jay's Grave.

A little beyond Swallerton Gate, on the way to Heatree Cross on the South East Moor, there is a burial mound where the road once divided. This is the grave of Kitty Jay, who hanged herself in the barn of a local farm nearly two hundred years ago.

Kitty was a young, unmarried workhouse girl brought to the farm as a drudge. Seduced by the son of the house, she took her own life and her body was interred at the crossroads. It was thought the devil could not claim a suicide's soul if the corpse was buried at a crossroads.

Fresh flowers in a jam jar are said to appear regularly on Kitty's grave overnight. In the summer with Hedge Barton's beeches catching the sunlight and the fireweed standing high on top of the drystone wall towards Heatree, the grave occupies a serene corner of the tourist circuit. Coaches pull in but there is little of the usual hasty clatter of people getting out. Cars stop, cameras click and people gather round and stare at the mound with its jar of willow herb.

Waiting behind a hot noon of crowded roads, sun-splashed hills and thatched cottages in villages, which have become lovely middle-class reservations, is the pub salad or the microwave pasty and the yellow commercial fizz which travels in cans under the label of 'cider'. And Jay's Grave is left to the birdsong and the hush of the surrounding pastures until the next coach slows to a halt.

Fox Tor Mire is another place, a place beyond the reach of coach parties and sightseers. It is an expanse of boggy ground at the top of the Swincombe Valley about three miles south of Princetown. Beyond Peat Cot and Whiteworks is Childe's Tomb, standing at the end of a walk few tourists take because it traverses desolation. There is nothing but spaciousness, sky, the heat-rippled landscape and larksong.

The tomb of Childe the hunter who froze to death on Foxtor Mire.

**Will Webber, Mr Fox-Pitt and Norman Mortimore
discussing a grass sale, Chapple, Gidleigh.**

The nineteenth-century cross on its solid plinth is a memorial to Childe the Hunter who might have been Ordulf, son of the eleventh-century Earl of Devon. Caught in a blizzard while out hunting, he killed his horse, cut open the carcass and burrowed into it to keep warm; but he was still frozen to death. Before dying he dipped his finger in the animal's blood and scrawled his will on some stones – which is really the last thing you want to do if you are freezing!

'They fyrste that fyndes and bringes me to my grave,
The Priorie of Plimstoke they shall have.'

The monks of Tavistock carried the body across the River Tavy for a Christian burial at the Abbey, and duly inherited some of Childe's lands.

Go there alone or with a friend or someone you love. The landscape is a benediction and in high summer can look like part of the African veldt.

A landscape one loves is more than a collection of physical features which strike a chord in the being. Heart-places help to liberate us from the trivia which bombards existence. When there is no human presence between myself and the moor I am happy, for solitary walking is an enduring joy; and at the busiest time of year even cultivated country can conjure up an unblemished morning or afternoon.

Walking from Manaton to Heatree Cross under Easdon Tor, the season assembles its images: a party of sweating cyclists; a man in cloth cap and overalls driving cattle; children on ponies; a couple of hikers with rucksacks. To the left is Hayne Down but straight ahead after Heatree Cross is the lane men made centuries ago and is now a long Nature trail.

When the hawthorn blossom has fallen the dark smell of ramsons is sandwiched between hedges full of blue alkanet, pink campion and the white stars of stitchwort. The hedges are tall and are spared the flail mower. They meet overhead, green and sun-flushed, with small pieces of the sky showing between the gaps in the leaves.

Beyond Heatree Down is Natsworthy Manor with the lane running on to

Pittpark under the ridge that is crowned with Honeybag Tor and Chinkwell Tor to the left and the valley of the East Webburn River on the right below Hamel Down. A cuckoo calls, wood pigeons croon but the buzzard floating over the fields is noiseless. Through woods of old trees, the lane passes Stouts Cottages and crosses the Webburn over a stone bridge. Masses of wild flowers choke the waysides and arriving in Widecombe one has a clear recollection of birdsong, colour broken by light and shade, and scents always to be associated with that walk.

It remains in the mind to be found again in the great stained-glass window in the church at Buckfast Abbey. The window is a summer vision in a summer place, a work of art in the large commercial complex which has grown around St Mary's Abbey on the River Dart east of Buckfastleigh. The church towers above the car parks, out-buildings and crowds of sightseers, with the monks as tourist officers.

There was a monastery here in the year 1,000 but it was destroyed during the reign of Henry VIII. Monks came back from France in 1882 but nothing was left standing. By chance they uncovered the foundations of the church and six men rebuilt it with local stone. It was started in 1906 and finished thirty-two years later, as a labour of love. The brother who had laid the first stone also laid the last.

The Benedictine Order insists that its followers work with their hands and at Buckfast the monks are employed in crafts and jobs necessary to the maintenance of the building. Commercialisation is inevitable and the gift shop and restaurant are part of a belief in work as a way to God, just as the church is central to the glorification of God. But industry also supplies bodily needs. Buckfast Tonic Wine, with its secret medicaments, is distributed worldwide. The three hundred acre farm, the boarding school for boys, the stained-glass window workshop and the bee keeping and sale of honey are examples of successful free enterprise; and the visitors who come to this curious mixture of the mediaeval and the modern are usually impressed. They depart with bottles of wine and jars of honey.

The monks were the pioneers of a new technique in stained-glass making. Their slab glass is given an intense sparkle, a crystalline quality achieved by fracturing it to form facets. It will catch the light even on a dull day and glow. Buckfast windows have gone to one hundred and fifty different churches, but rivalling the production of superb glass is the bee keeping and the work in this field of Brother Adam, who is a world authority.

At Sherberton, in the lower Swincombe Valley, are the hives of the only bee breeding station in the British Isles. The apiary ensures pure mating and as it is right in the middle of the wilderness no other bees are about. It has operated since 1925.

Over the past seventy years the Buckfast bee keepers have produced a species strain which is industrious, good-tempered, fecund and disease resistant. Brother Adam says there are forty different characteristics he has to bear in mind when he makes the necessary selection and crosses. Each colony is highly individual and the quality of the honey varies. In the last few years Dartmoor has failed beekeepers due to the appalling weather.

But most summers when the heather is purple bees will be busy providing another of those soothing wilderness voices.

LEISURE

The sun sets, starlight floods Dartmoor, then the sun rises again and presently the hang-gliders are swinging across the morning above Widgery Cross near Lydford. Against the sun glare in black silhouette they are noiseless, giant dragonflies swooping and cruising in wonderful defiance of gravity.

Water sports on Meldon Reservoir prompt a 'value judgement'. All the Dartmoor reservoirs are potential Nature reserves of great value. In themselves they constitute the taking from the moor. Giving the water back to wildlife would be compensation and enrichment. Leisure activities are obtrusive. They disturb wildfowl and remove another wildlife 'Elsewhere'. Elsewheres are those mysterious places which animals, birds and insects are expected to colonise when they are dispossessed of their normal habitat. Developers and others would have us believe there is a surfeit of such 'places'. But habitat loss equals creature loss and one day we are going to run out of Elsewheres.

Rock climbing is a wilderness activity. Providing the climbers respect the seasonal requirement of nesting birds and do not remove vegetation to make gulleys and cracks easier to ascend, they do little harm. I've always hated the sound of pitons being hammered home in granite. For me it was vandalism far worse than the discarded drinks can or the crumpled crisp packet chucked among the bog moss.

Climbing demands physical effort allied to skill and fitness. The joy and thrill of setting hand to rock is difficult to share with non-climbers. It is the celebration of the tactile, a fingertip knowledge of the vertical moor. Afterwards, when it is over, to sit on a tor and survey the landscape from that marvellous glow of well-being is among life's most satisfying experiences. But the opportunity to separate oneself from man's activities on the moors is as important as the provision of activities for man on the moors.

For me the preservation of solitude means the continued safe existence of the moor's wildlife. I would willingly relinquish the privilege of walking to places like Fur

Tor and Red Lake or anywhere else if those areas were changing due to an increase in human activity.

Pony trekking, which may seem to be one of the few truly harmonious leisure activities on the moors, is, in fact, a cause for concern. The mounted farmer or a couple of riders exercising their horses bring the landscape to life, but pony trekking has grown from those posses of bright-faced novices enjoying their first gallop on the downs, to regular cavalry charges over regular routes. The consequent erosion is ugly and the granite tramway on Haytor Down is an example of the damage caused by hooves cutting into the turf, day after day, throughout the spring, summer and autumn.

The Dartmoor National Park Authority is concerned about the protection of Dartmoor and the difficulties of helping people to enjoy it properly. The Park Authority has existed since 1951 and the Dartmoor Park Committee have 'the right under county bylaws to prosecute for the scattering of litter, feeding of animals, or unlawful lighting of fires'. Their approach is persuasive rather than aggressive. The Dartmoor user is encouraged to cooperate with the professionals in preserving the beauty of the wilderness. The public's cooperation is vital, but when it comes to hard vandalism the Park's forces haven't the teeth to protect sensitive areas. They could not, for instance, match the political clout and financial fire power of landowners like the Duchy of Cornwall or the Forestry Commission if ever there were serious confrontations. The Duchy owns 70,000 acres of National Park. It is immensely powerful; but since the Dartmoor Commons Act of 1985, the public have the right of access to a hundred thousand acres of common land. Maybe this will produce a shift in the balance of power.

Aloof from conflict is the season itself. The grass waving on the high moor can never quite hide the bones and scraps of wool and the mummified bodies of pony mares. The sedge grass grows in tussocks and its green blades are loved by all free-running livestock. Soon those tussocks will turn yellow and the animals will have to cover a wider range for their food; but for a while the greenness is life-giving and seemingly endless.

Above: Arthur Brown shearing by hand
at Moor Gate.
Right: Richard Leaman power shearing
at Waye Down.

WORKING LIFE AND PLAY

Thatching is one of those rural crafts that reaches deep into the moor's past. There are examples of it all over the National Park from the showpiece cottages of Buckland in the Moor to North Bovey and Lustleigh, and other villages of the in-country. The thatcher earns good money for the hard graft and skill that goes into the creation of the Olde Worlde Charm eagerly sought by those tourists pursuing the rustic idyll. Thatch is as practical as it is attractive; it dulls noise and gives cool rooms in summer and a warm house in winter.

Roofing a cottage in traditional style, the thatcher secures the bundles, or yealms, of straw to the roof timbers, working from the eaves to the ridge. The slats are gradually covered as he shakes out the yealms and pegs them down, layer by layer in overlapping ascent. He works with iron hooks, hand shears, a shearing hook, sparhook and the leggat or 'bat' for shaping the straw. The dull gold of new thatch, gleaming from summer rain, is comforting after a morning on the open moor.

There is romance in farmwork and stonewalling and other forms of manual labour when viewed from a coach window. The sight of sheepdogs going about their job is something most folk can't resist. Sheep round-ups occur throughout the year for various reasons: shearing, dipping, vaccination, tupping and market.

In the summer the Scottish Blackfaces of the high moor and the down-country flocks of Dartmoors or Closewools, also grazing the common, are brought in to be dipped against scab. They have about them a stiff urgency, but a few collies cope where an army of men would be hard pressed to prevent the mass scattering.

Throughout the moor sheep are gathered. Figures on horseback and the black and white dogs move purposefully to steer the animals down into the dipping pens and the chemically-laced baths. The sheep are pushed under and thoroughly soaked and the tang of dip spreads on the air that is loud with bleating. Thin, wet-looking creatures stagger from the bath, blinking, and shaking themselves and smelling strong.

The Olde Worlde Charm of Buckland in the Moor.

The sheepdog trials are events which bring the Dartmoor farming community together with experts appraising the work of other experts' dogs in a friendly atmosphere. The sanguine manoeuvring of sheep by collies into pens is much more than entertainment. It is emulation of the wilderness happening where patience, restraint and experience are essential to the gathering; and a good dog is worth its weight in gold.

Each collie has to show his worth in a series of tests, all linked to moor work and positive shepherding. The Outrun leads to the Lift, the Fetch, the Drive and the Shedding and, ultimately, the Penning. Each stage examines the qualities and character of the dog which are revealed by the way he handles the little group of sheep.

The collie's temperament is important. If he is restless and too eager he may make the sheep nervous and increase the difficulty of his task. Steadiness and mental and physical agility are all apparent in the champion. To witness his skill on the high moor beneath summer clouds, with the sheep leaving the hillsides in white streams, is to add a few unforgettable moments to a Dartmoor holiday. Widecombe Fair is also unforgettable for different reasons.

I sat on a rock on the hill above the valley of the East Webburn and the village. The mist did not look as if it had any intention of lifting. The houses and church far below were masked and only the walled fields climbing the flanks of Hamel Down suggested there was more to the scene than heather and bracken.

At Widecombe the countryside is beautiful and the lap of the valley has been farmed to hill-country perfection. Throughout the early hours of that September morning traffic had been creeping down the road into the mist: horseboxes, vans, lorries, cars crammed with boxes, packages and bundles. Invisibly below, Widecombe Fair was beginning its annual resurrection. Stalls and sideshows were being assembled on the green and farmstock was arriving at the field beyond the vicarage.

When the church tower emerged from the thinning greyness and the sun shone from a blue sky that grew larger by the moment, the traffic had increased to a steady, nose-to-tail crawl. Charabancs and cars crept down towards the rooftops of the village that had materialised. Now Widecombe had become the melting pot of West Country tourism. Down there the holiday season was being laid to rest with gusto and vulgarity. The fair was a wake for the dead summer but as I joined the traffic queue it was comforting to know that the wind was sweeping across acres of solitude just over the hill.

Widecombe Fair is a pageant in two parts. The first is mid-Atlantic – loud, brash, geared to the spending and making of money. The second is the rural dream watered by genuine enthusiasm and succeeding because it is an authentic reflection of moorland life. The two, alas, aren't separate entities. They feed on each other.

The origins of the Fair go back over five hundred years. In former times the only holidays were feast days or fair days. Fifteenth-century law demanded archery practice during the festivities and on Buttes Park, Widecombe's village green, every able-bodied man was obliged to shoot arrows at standard targets or buttes. The legendary Tom Cobley would have been on his way to a fair that once began in this fashion.

The Tom Cobley phenomenon, with all its commercial spin-offs, put Widecombe on the tourist map, but he didn't live in the village and never even reached it on the famous old grey mare. A ballad and a catchy tune settled Widecombe's fate.

I found the green covered in stalls and carousels. The most unlikely stuff was on offer to the crowds – cheap toys and trinkets, jacket potatoes, T-shirts, sticky fudge, fortune telling, ice creams, balloons, fairground spiel, hot dogs and souvenirs. The stink of fried food hung over the place. It was noisy, hot, slightly hysterical and catch-penny.

In the nearby churchyard tired day-trippers sat with backs to gravestones, dozing, while family groups beseiged the pony mares and foals. The Women's Institute soon sold out of homemade pasties, sandwiches, scones and fruit cake, but the ladies continued brewing tea. The pub was packed with drinkers eager to pit their capacity against the dreaded scrumpy which loosens kneecaps, teeth and bowels.

Through the gates into the showground the scene changed. The field had about it the smell of animals. Penned ewes were being eyed-up by farmers, and the rams tethered by the horn to the fence were obviously unhappy. They panted in the heat that had some of the young men discarding their shirts.

Behind a marquee I found the handbell ringers of Moretonhampstead Primary School performing. Next door the St John's Ambulance brigaders were tucking into salads and the refreshment tent was catering for most thirsts, alcoholic and otherwise. I sauntered past the sheep-shearing demonstration and the line of vintage tractors to watch the show-jumping. Girls in jodhpurs were coaxing their ponies through the delicious ordeals of the gymkhana.

As it grew hotter, the pure-bred Dartmoor ponies and Shetlands followed the big work horses onto the parade to receive rosettes or nothing, according to how they looked to the judges. Then the foxhounds, the huntsman and the master made a dramatic entrance and sixteen and a half couples of hounds lolloped about. The crowd was called in and there was a spontaneous get-together of animals and people.

Perhaps the most enduring memory of the day was the sight of a shire horse in its show brasses. There are few things in nature to compare with the singing glint of brass as an animal seventeen and a half hands high trots before an admiring crowd.

In the end I could dismiss the mess on the green as a bit of chaos thrown in to heighten the pleasure of the agricultural show. Widecombe Fair remains the family outing, the chance for the townee to share some of the traditional country pastimes moor-folk take for granted. Awful commercialisation has somehow managed an unholy marriage with bona fide rural charm. Once a year is probably just about right.

The heather at the roadside is purple and the whortleberries have been picked for the pie-making. Fewer bathers take to the water in Haytor Quarry pools and Tavy Cleave. The rowans are clustered with bright scarlet berries. The radiant green hillsides of early summer are dark now. Insects rise from the tall bracken and house martins fly back and forth over the ponds. But the in-country swifts departed weeks ago. The hoof prints of cattle at Holwell Farm are silvered with spiders' webs as fine as mist.

Dew lies just that little longer in field corners and there are vacancy signs outside the B and B establishments. Most of the tourists have gone and what have they left behind; an empty coke can, a cigarette packet, the faint smell of petrol fumes, lots of money in the tills of the moorland shops, cafes, pubs and hotels? And what did they take away – souvenirs, fudge, a garden pixie? It would be easy to dismiss the casual visit to Dartmoor in these cynical, condescending terms. But I believe Richard Jefferies was right when he wrote: 'The hills purify those who walk on them.'

Even that stroll from the car park onto Hay Tor or a jaunt on Pork Hill brings an individual or a family into the truth of Jefferies' philosphy.

Dartmoor does give something to the spirit; and I like to think that in the winter, in an industrial city, a man or woman will look up from an unpleasant task and recall the vision of a sunlit tor or a field of cotton grass waving in the wind or cloud massing over blue hills.

I'm glad the diluted spirit of the moors is enough for most visitors, because that's the only way the wilderness can survive for selfish wilderness addicts like myself to enjoy! Whatever happens, though, the value of the place as a tourist attraction or a lone walker's haven should never take priority over its global importance. It is a unique corner of the living world.

AUTUMN

FLOCKING BIRDS FILL THE SKY,
DAYS SHORTEN AND SHADOWS LENGTHEN
AND GALES SUDDENLY GIVE WAY
TO MORNINGS OF WINDLESS CALM.

Previous page: The pony drift at Chagford Common.

UPSTREAM

Autumn begins to edit the landscape. The evening sun conjures amazing hues from the hills and woods; old gold, browns, yellows, bronze, a splash of crimson and scarlet against dark masses of heather. Tors vanish into the sky as the mist thickens to snuff out the larksong and leave just the clatter of a stream running across the odours of decay.

Wherever there are trees Renaissance colour flares but the oaks of the river valleys of the Meavy, Teign, Walkham and Dart do not glow as they did in the spring. The moor is acquiring its loneliness character. Flocking birds fill the sky, days shorten and shadows lengthen and gales suddenly give way to mornings of windless calm. Great drifts of leaves cover the road near the cattle grid above Holwell Lawn where the beech trees grow in the old stone wall on the western side.

Autumn is the time of the Apple Moon, St Luke's Little Summer, cider making, the tupping and the pony drifts. Where the houses end and the fields begin, birds are stripping the hedges of hips and haws. The blackthorn is stippled with bullens and bracken is the colour of a fox. But, even after a frosty night, a fine day will climb to the sundance of butterflies, and buzzards will be on the wing above coombes whose rivers are brimful.

The life of the countryside is in the sky and the water, and the overlapping of the prehistoric and modern belongs to the ephemera of human existence. Yet this remains an occult landscape. As the winter thrushes pour in from the high latitudes there is an awareness of living in Nature and of the interplay between people, the environment and the seasons. Pagan things survive in the blood and in ritual. Earth Mother lives on as the Virgin Mary; the Beltane Fires burn every November 5th, re-christened Guy Fawkes' bonfires but of ancient significance. The old needs endure – the need to call up the spirits of grain, sun and water; the need to exact promises from Nature in the mist and leaf-fall, with endings conspicuous and a growing awareness of mortality shared with plants and animals.

Sammy Harris collecting his stallion at Yardworthy pony drift.

The beauty of autumn for primitive man was also the edge of crisis. Maybe the itch to get up and go which attacks many people in October is the memory of some fundamental desire to avoid what lies beyond November. Maybe it is instinct recalling the Ice Ages and winters which seemed to last forever.

On Dartmoor one can become part of a splendour noticeably absent from most human affairs. The total experience of the wilderness brings this home – trees, grass, hills, sky, wildlife, water, distant horizons, weather and the minutiae available on any wilderness walk. Hold a piece of frosted lichen to the sun and wonder grows. Watch the pony running before an autumn shower with the grass and bracken soaked in sunshine and rain, and sanctity of life suddenly has marvellous relevance.

Few spectacles compare with a Dartmoor dusk when the starling flocks come roaring over Belstone Common. That smoking, fade-away of day can hollow the stomach and leave a kind of homesickness for a place yet to be visited. Then stand in a Bench Tor twilight and wait for the brilliance of the night sky to overwhelm Devon, and perhaps you will start to think about creation and the animal life that is flesh and blood and capable of responding to the beauty of place and season.

Between snags of heather the separate strands spun by spiders lift in the wind and flow as undulations of light up the hillside. The smell of the swaling fires and the chirr of crickets belong to the dusks which Devonians call dimpsey. Barn owl October of huge moons becomes colder November with pubs too warm and sociable to resist. There will be the chance to toast legs still a little dead from the wind and rain of high moor walking before real log fires or gas forgeries, while the regulars play that most celtic of card games, Euchre.

Bees and wasps are at the ivy flower and the flocks of lapwings, chaffinches, rooks, redwings and fieldfares pass over the in-country. Everywhere wild animals are over-eating, building up body fat for the winter months. Ten thousand woodpigeons will eat nearly fifteen hundredweight of kernels as they swarm to the beechmast.

The leaf-fall colours of decline spill from the in-country across the moor to the bracken and solitary rowans and hawthorns and onto the three upland deciduous

Above: The buzzard, Dartmoor's ever-present bird of prey.
Right: Joe White at his 'Taddy Pit', Batworthy Farm.

copses of Black Tor Beare, Piles Copse and Wistman's Wood. The rivers are in spate, roaring full and wild down from the high moor. At Bellever, above the broken clapper bridge and the road bridge, there is a coppery gleam of salmon in the water. Sweeping away the frost, the mild south westerly winds have brought rain to Dartmoor. Rivers and streams have risen and the salmon are running. They will push up streams like the Cherry Brook and rivers like the East Dart to spawning beds in reaches a pony can jump.

The autumn run of salmon is among Dartmoor's most thrilling spectacles. The Game Fish are capable of leaping over ten feet in their desire to reach the 'redds' where the eggs are laid. Big adults leave the spate in a curving explosion of burnished red. The fish knifing through the current under the compulsion of instinct are another expression of the life force. Those leaping at Bellever are brothers and sister sharing a common desire to return to the spawning grounds where they were hatched. A female can lay upwards of 20,000 eggs and even heavy predation leaves enough fry to maintain enormous 'kin-groups' with their particular stretch of moorland water.

The life cycle of the salmon is astonishing. It begins at the redds. Twisting and shuddering the female uses her body and tail to dig a hollow (a 'redd') in the riverbed gravel up to a foot deep. Then with the cock fish at her side, she lays her eggs and he looses his milt. The eggs are swept into the grit and gravel and the mating fish move upstream and repeat the process. So the grit from the fresh excavation covers the eggs previously deposited. Throughout the upper waters of the Cherry Brook, where the stream is shallow, the tell-tale signs are visible – the pits, grooves and mounds.

The alevins hatch out in March and early April and emerge from the redds about a month later. Yolk paunches drained, the fry find life hazardous as they shoot around the shallows picking off minute aquatic creatures. At a year old they are called parr and have distinctive brown and red spotted bodies. When the spots vanish beneath silver, the parr has become a smolt and sooner or later the migratory urge turns it towards the sea which provides abundant food to accelerate growth. The young of many other fish fill the salmon's stomach as it hunts the ocean. It can remain feasting on sea food for six months or several years but at some moment the mating instinct draws the fish back, amazingly and mysteriously, to its home estuary.

Here various groups of both sexes congregate, preparing for the spawning runs. Some are grilse – youngsters making the run after about a year at sea. With them will be 'mended kelts' that have made perhaps several journeys to and from the spawning beds. Sheathed in the lustre of well-being the big fish are torpedoes of energy. When conditions are right they battle upsteam to guarantee the survival of their kind. Some have lurked in pools for months waiting for the water temperature to trigger off the run; others come straight into the race or delay their run until early winter. All have lost their silver coats during the waiting period in fresh water.

The males have dulled to a red-mottled copper with large dark spots and have hooked lower jaws. They are now known as 'reds'. The hens are a darker hue and negotiate the torrents above the bridges of Bellever or Factory Bridge on the Teign at Chagford under the collective title of 'black' fish. The river in spate, leaping salmon and the golden glow of the surrounding countryside combine to create yet another of those visions which are the quintessence of autumn Dartmoor.

DOWN THE LEAT

Over the slow lift of hill the clouds are rolling out their thunder. Water froths off granite on its way into the streams and rivers and leats. Then the big anvil-headed clouds pass and blue sky fills the gap between storms. The sky is exerting its power on the landscape. The juxtaposition of light and shade produces an illusion of movement. Colour strengthens to a warm glow then fades to drabness, but water on the move always catches the eye.

Leats may lack the charisma of rivers and upland streams, but they possess an appeal of their own. These narrow, artificial water-courses were engineered along the contours of open, hilly country and today many of them continue to make dignified descents from source to destination. In some places they still supply water for farmstock and domestic use; but in the past they were also essential to many of the industries based on the moor. Water power continues to play an important part in the industrial life of the area, but once it was everything.

The Grimstone and Sortridge Leat is taken from the River Walkham at Grimstone Head Weir. The farm under Little Mis Tor draws its drinking water and livestock water from it, and Merrivale Quarry also taps it to cool the saws that cut the granite blocks. This is the only working quarry left on Dartmoor proper, and maybe the increased demand for granite kerbstones will keep it in operation for years to come. Its impact on the surrounding countryside is devastating. Noise, dust and the coming and going of heavy vehicles create an atmosphere entirely alien to the peacefulness of the Walkham Valley.

At Merrivale Quarry it is possible to sit on London Bridge – well, part of it anyway. The blocks were cut from moorland granite in the last century and came home to Dartmoor. A rich American actually bought the bridge and made arrangements to have it sent in pieces to the States. Obviously it would have been impractical to ship all the masonry, so facings were cut off the blocks ready to be set on a concrete structure. The job was done and the bridge re-assembled in the Arizona Desert. Then the excited

Right: **Foggintor Quarry, one of the many abandoned quarries being reclaimed by Nature.**

Above: Cattle grazing in the warm glow of evening under Gutter Tor.
Right: Dick Able separating his stock in the Merrivale drift pound.

Devonport Leat above the West Dart River and Wistman's Wood.

The engine house of disused Wheal Betsy on Black Down above Mary Tavy.

entrepreneur came along to inspect his prize but when he saw it his jaw dropped. He had indeed bought London Bridge, but expected to see Tower Bridge which most Americans regard as London Bridge. But despite this bit of costly ignorance the crowds still flock to see the Dartmoor granite in that unlikely setting. The blocks which yielded the facings remain at Merrivale not far from the road.

The Grimstone and Sortridge Leat flows on, bringing water to the animals of more farms below Merrivale until it returns to the Walkham again. Running shallow over beds of stone and grit, leats are nearly always autumn-coloured browns and bronze. Lee Moor Leat which carries water to the English China Clay Works from the River Plym is no exception. It glides over the countryside from the upper reaches of the river into the sprawl of white waste tips, buildings and mica lagoons of this busy site. But the landscape of Lee Moor is losing its corpse glow as the works gradually melt back into the borderland of the moors. Although the slow process won't satisfy some environmentalists, there is a comforting inevitability about it.

China clay is necessary to modern life and on Dartmoor kaolin deposits are found in granite. They are decomposed felspars which have rotted down to powder, and the brightness and whiteness of Lee Moor's clay make it a very commercial product. The bulk of it is exported to sixty different countries. As with all Dartmoor's traditional industries, water is integral to the business. It is used to extract the clay and has helped form one of the most dramatic of Dartmoor's man-made landscapes of sandhills, lakes and pits.

Giant water hoses called monitors blast the clay from the sides of the pits, at a pressure of 1,500 gallons a minute and create in their mist on the white screen of the cliff an astonishing play of rainbows. Each jet is powerful enough to knock over a double-decker bus. They sweep with an explosive roar along the face, eating into it and sending it crashing to the ground in crumbling masses. To separate the clay from the emulsified cliff, giant Archimedes screws like terrible war machines from a novel by H.G. Wells, extract the heavy sand, leaving the clay and mica.

There are ten tons of sand for every ton of china clay. The little beach at Saltash on the Tamar originated at Lee Moor. Unfortunately the works are too far from large cities to make the transport of this good building sand viable, so the tips continue to grow. They are no longer conical. Regulations introduced after the Aberfan disaster have led to 'benching' and the changed face of that once 'lunar landscape'. The newer benched mounds are being grassed over and greenness is creeping over the workings. The mounds have become habitat for plants, insects and small mammals, including rabbits and voles. Buzzards and kestrels hunt the slopes and foxes thrive here.

Even the mica lagoons, which are lovely blue and silver lakes, where the glittering mica settles after the clay has been removed and before the water is returned to the river, have become bird sanctuaries attracting wildfowl like Canada geese, and gulls, waders and lapwings. Yet, behind the greening of Lee Moor, is a series of disturbing images – white tips running with water and white crags disintegrating under great jets of water, heavy lorries roaring back and forth over off-white roads and churned-up tracks; pits and complexes of machinery and buildings covered in white grime. This is the paraphernalia of an operation which supplies some of the requirements of the pharmaceutical, paints and plastic industries as well as china clay's best-known product – a filler for paper. Out of the white chaos of noise and continual activity comes the gloss of a quality magazine.

Some day in the future Lee Moor will die as an ugly commercial concern. Then it could become a wildlife paradise of lakes, marshes and small hills. Maybe those moral horizons aren't so distant after all, if we advance towards them by attempting to re-establish genuine wilderness character in the places we have ruined through exploitation. Amenities, the opportunity for leisure activities and other ways a landscape can be brought under the thumb even in the attempt to cover up industrial vandalism, have no place in this great upland.

Meanwhile the leats continue to wind across autumn silences often unnoticed by the casual visitor. Holystreet Leat is among the most inconspicuous. At Chagford it makes a stealthy exit from some trees near Chagford Bridge. A gate opens onto an enclosed yard with a sluice and a funny little building no bigger than a garage. In the

Top: Bowerman's Nose stands surrounded by legend on Hayne Down.
Bottom: The stone circle at the end of the long stone row, Erme Plains.

autumn the pool behind the building is braided with fallen leaves and full of trout. Winged insects sail over it as the leat flows from the pool and the hounds in the nearby hunt kennels start belling. The Electricity Generating Board has power stations and generating stations the size of villages feeding the National Grid. At Chagford Bridge, Holystreet Leat is supplying the tiny 'garage' of a hydro-electric station with enough water to keep it ticking over. It produces electricity for no more than thirty one-bar electric fires. This corner-shop business principle can still be accommodated on Dartmoor where the British genius for thinking small is manifested in the most unlikely places. Well, it's pleasant now and then to be reminded that God created the 'Garden' of Eden not the Grand Canyon of Eden!

The theory behind leats is wonderfully simple – gravity, the contour descent, water flowing over granite, rarely in a hurry. A fine example, the Devonport Leat runs across ravishing wilderness country. It was conceived to bring water to the naval town of Dock which later became Devonport. Work began in 1793 and the leat took three years to cut but continued to do its job until 1898 when Burrator Reservoir was built.

The leat begins at the weir above Wistman's Wood on the West Dart and curves around the flank of Beardown to take in the Cowsic at Beardown Farm and the Blackbrook at Princetown. Beyond Tor Royal, it flows to Whiteworks and on underground through a tunnel near Nun's Cross. Bubbling out into the sunlight again, it seems to run uphill above the remains of an old mine working, Crazywell Pool. Then with uncharacteristic gusto it comes stumbling and roaring white off Raddick Hill to cross the River Meavy by way of an iron launder en route to its present destination – Burrator Reservoir. In the last century the leat made a Homeric descent of nearly thirty miles from its West Dart source to Devonport. Now it covers a modest nine or ten miles but ends up in the same place – piped from Burrator.

DUSK

The tupping brings the ewes and rams together. From these unions the seeds of next year's lamb crop are sown. So the pageant of decay is part of the landscape's repertoire of beautiful seasonal deceptions. Autumn is a period of change and investment in the future. Yet old anomalies go unchecked and the shortcomings of some of the people involved in animal husbandry will begin to register as the weather deteriorates. Animals as money on the hoof are the harsh reality of the Dartmoor idyll throughout the year, but their lot can be improved. In Nature life passes to life — rabbit to buzzard, vole to kestrel, weakling lamb to fox. There is a dignity in the blood-letting of predators which is often absent from man's casual venality or his use of farmstock.

At dusk people vanish from the open moor, leaving the place to the wild creatures, the sheep, ponies and cattle. It is the clicketting time of the fox and the vixen screams her eerie mating cry to be answered by the barks of dog foxes running in to compete for her favours. Few sounds capture so well the mood of the autumn landscape.

On Hayne Down, south of Manaton, is a granite stack nearly forty feet high, a vertical rock formation standing not far from the roadside like a pagan idol. To crouch on its small summit listening to foxes call across Cripdon Down with evening fading and the sun and moon briefly sharing the sky, is an experience never to be forgotten.

Bowerman's Nose is a granite pile wrapped in myth, legend and fanciful absurdity. Here Bowerman ('Bowman', the hunter and archer) is said to have been magicked to stone by a party of local witches. His hounds ran on as far as Hound Tor where the spell caught up with them and they became dog-shaped rocks. The assumption that Bowerman is a derivation of the Welsh fawr-maen, great stone (pronounced vawr-maen), does not hold water. Old Welsh was the tongue of Celtic Britain but in that language the adjective comes after the noun, giving us 'maen-fawr'.

Foxes pad around places like Hayne Down unimpressed by the peculiar human habit of bequeathing so many aspects of the natural world with supernatural qualities. To a fox a rock is a rock and a sunset merely a brightness in the bottom of the sky, and each season is a journey in search of food.

When a cock salmon, with his hooked lower jaw, dies at the end of the spawning run, the dog fox will come to the head waters of the river and feast on the emaciated carcass. The fox lives on the edge of the mires close to a stump of granite which merlins use as a slab for butchering songbirds. The little falcons catch larks and meadow pipits in flight and break them up on this post.

The big foreign thrushes passing over the mires and Hayne Down plunder the rowan berries and haws. Round, cold eyes mirror the browns and golds of the season. The eyes of the thrush family seem devoid of feeling. They remind me of prehistory, when winged reptiles hunted the wastes and that merciless gaze settled on some cowering creature. Fish bones, animal bones, crumbling sunlight, grasses and reeds withering, the barking of foxes and the sound of moorland streams; some elements of Dartmoor are changeless. We take possession of the place as the place takes possession of us; and there is truth in the assertion that the pastoral instinct can recognise what reason overlooks.

Yet despite its massive presence the moors' prehistory has a curious anonymity, as if the human element of Neolithic and Bronze Age times is crushed beneath the stones of successive cultures. The longhouse, the tin miner's hut and the derelict farm buildings move us because human associations are strong. Maybe a child's initials are cut into a window ledge or above the hearth, and one recognises the spirits of individual beings. The laughter of a family at the fireside or the suffering of the labouring class endures wherever there are roofless shells with windows and doors.

A circle of stones only occasionally summons up a vision of the life of pre-literate people. Yet Dartmoor is rich in antiquities and hundreds of important sites mark the remains of some of the country's oldest buildings. Granite will have its say, although the voice of the distant past is faint and never that of the individual.

On the South Moor is probably the longest stone row in the world. For over two miles the row runs from the Erme Plains on Stall Moor to Green Hill. When a November day closes there, calmly and noiselessly, the stones brew their own atmosphere which the imaginative may find vaguely disturbing. Then the darkening wilderness can seem the loneliest place in the world. Also on Stall Moor, north of New Waste and Cornwood, is probably the most impressive stone row. The stones are tall and sweep the gaze up into the wilderness and the mind back in time. Unlike metal and earthenware artefacts which the acid soil destroys, granite raised by our ancestors has weathered well. The kistvaens, cromlechs, pounds, reaves, hut circles, standing stones and stone rows constitute a cipher of prehistory.

The drystone walls are part of the more immediate past and the present. Heavy at the base, flat on one side and knobbly on the other, they are handsome filigree structures. They suit the place, although to run up against one in the mist at the end of a long walk, can be frustrating. The craftsmen who built them have written a chapter of their own lives on the hillsides; but the mated foxes trotting beside the boundary wall by South Hessary Tor are aware only of each other and what the dusk holds. They will leave their musk in warm pockets on the night and listen to the thin contact calls of the redwings as the flocks continue to cross the stars near the end of their migration flights.

QUARRIES, MINES AND CONIES

The disused quarry a few hundred yards north of Hay Tor is a monument to the demand for granite in the last century. Even the tramway, which carried the stone to the Stover Canal and the barge which took it to the schooners moored at Teignmouth dock, had granite rails cut like hefty kerbstones. Stone from here was used to rebuild London Bridge but Queen Victoria had been on the throne for less than fifteen years when the industry slumped.

Many churches owe their beauty and durability to some of the moor's four hundred varieties of granite, and famous landmarks like Nelson's Column were once part of the Devon wilderness. Merrivale Quarry supplied stone for the building of New Scotland Yard thirty years ago and from rock quarries around Foggin Tor, Princetown came into being.

The moor is covered with clues to the part played by granite in history. Mortar stones, crosses, aqueducts, grindstones, rollers, gateposts, water troughs, cider presses, clapper bridges and the houses and drystone walls which keep cropping up, can be found among the ruins of prehistory. They are now familiar and, on the whole, acceptable parts of Dartmoor, but Meldon Quarry near Okehampton is growing even larger.

Meldon is on the edge of the National Park. It supplies ballast to the Western and Southern Regions of British Rail. Ballast is the non-granite stone required to maintain a base for sleeper and railway lines. At Meldon, quarrying is a massive operation involving science-fiction machinery and vehicles with wheels that dwarf a man. The process of making ballast is simple. It starts with a deep-throated underground explosion. The ground shudders and lifts in a surge that can send upwards of 20,000 tons of rock rolling forward from the face, exactly as planned. Giant dumper trucks cart away the debris to the crushing machine high in the quarry. Here rocks are pulverised and spewed out as ballast. Freight trains constantly arrive and depart, on rails set in ballast to collect ballast for other rails as the old stuff is ground down by high-speed trains.

Above: Drystone walling at Teignhead Newtake.
Right: The granite tramway once used to carry stone to the Stover Canal.

Meldon has operated for decades, employing the muscle and skill of generations of Okehampton men, and is obviously vital to the town's economy.

A recent survey showed that every individual in the USA requires ten pounds of explosives a year to supply them with their mineral needs. The environmentalists who drive to Meldon to protest about the operation, travel on roads quarried from stone, in cars made from minerals, powered by petrol which is also extracted from the earth. Meldon is on the fringe of Dartmoor, yet without watchfulness and environmentalist pressure the wilderness could surrender some of its finest areas to similar projects.

In the long term I believe Meldon will return quietly to the moor, probably as a nature reserve centred on a reservoir. Despite the good intentions of such a scheme it would be out of place in a wilder area. 'Nature reserve' usually means paths, signposts, facilities, order, neatness – everything the wilderness can do without. Perhaps Hay Tor Quarry is closer to nature now because it has looked after itself since it was abandoned. Rowans and ferns sprout from crags where birds nest. The twin pools boast lillies and dragonflies. The place is soft on the eye and rich with colour and wildlife in the autumn and spring.

'Elsewheres' continue to dwindle. Maybe we shall not know the real value of the lark until it has vanished forever from the autumn morning along with the landscape necessary to it existence.

But the living world creeps back to cover the scars industry leaves behind as it fails. When autumn closes it is possible to walk through solitude only to step into an industrialised corner of the moors. At first it may not be apparent, then you notice something about the landscape that isn't quite right. The gullies may have an artificial regularity and the heather-clad hummocks are evenly distributed among pools and paths. For centuries man has exploited the high wilderness and Nature has followed in his wake, re-clothing the bare earth and rock with bracken, grass, heather, whortle-berry and furze. Beauty has grown out of dereliction.

Since the Bronze Age tin was hacked and washed from the ground and Dartmoor was once the richest source of that mineral in Europe. Early tinners were 'streaming' for ore in the days when smelting was primitive. They went up rivers' narrowing reaches by embanking the flow and collecting the black stones washed from the lodes. 'Blowing-houses' made smelting easier and more efficient. The advance of knowledge meant large quantities of tin could be extracted. The blowing-houses beside streams, with their waterwheels to work the bellows of the furnaces, are a feature of rivers like the Meavy at Black Tor Falls. Leats and launders were nearly always necessary to create the fall of water required to turn the small waterwheel. At Black Tor Falls are mortar stones hollowed with what look like giant thumb-prints which were the result of the stamps employed to crush the tin gravel.

The old opencast workings which dug along the lodes, sometimes with the odd shaft, were replaced by true shaft mining in the early 18th century. By the end of that century mechanical advances led to further mining development, although production could not match the boom years of the Middle Ages. It was possible to cut horizontally through the side of the hill or a man-made gully into the vein of tin. Vertical shafts required drainage by pumping (instead of the traditional adits), with the use of giant waterwheels driven by leats which also supplied the power for the crushing and dressing machines.

The beehive huts of miners' caches, the wheel pits, the 'buddles' or circular troughs, where ore sand was washed, blowing-houses and wheel houses, are reminders of an industry which changed vast areas of moorland. Without water the business could not have thrived and the tell-tale mining landscape would be different. What may look natural was once a roaring, bustling industrial concern and the site around Birch Tor, east of the Warren House Inn and the Postbridge–Moretonhampstead Road, is typical of a group of busy mine workings: Birch Tor and Vitifer, and Golden Dagger, all close to Headland Warren where the land is furrowed with gulleys and ravines. Vitifer was served by a seven mile leat taken from the East Dart. It could boast a shaft four hundred and twenty feet deep.

There was the constant activity of men and horses with the din of machinery carrying for miles. The earth was laid bare and bled of its wealth; but today the workings

Beware of the dog at Roundhill, Two Bridges.

are part of the downs which fall to Soussons Plantation. The shells of the industry and even the spoil heaps are sightly. In reclothing dereliction, Nature has created something delightful but here like so many other places man's past and the life of the moors remain difficult to separate. Perhaps this is characteristic of the whole of Britain.

The white flash of scuts as rabbits shoot into the undergrowth under Birch Tor opens another of those windows on Dartmoor's past. Headland Warren with its walled enclosures occupied nearly six hundred acres. The warrener's house and its kennels stood at the head of the Challacombe Valley. In this and similar warrens such as Huntingdon, Ditsworthy and Trowlesworthy, rabbits were bred for the table. The animals dug their buries in aritificial banks or pillow mounds sometimes within stone walls. Throughout autumn and winter, men and dogs drove the rabbits into nets and killed them. The carcasses went to market and the dried skins to the furriers. Stone vermin traps were created to thwart stoats and weasels. The warreners have gone but the conies remain, in smaller numbers, and wherever there are clitters there are buries. On an autumn evening the rabbits can be seen on the turf under Birch Tor taking the last of the sun. Some fall prey to the stoats, foxes and buzzards which hunt the valley of the West Webburn where it flows between hillsides of heather past Soussons conifer plantation.

Soussons attracts birds and birdwatchers. During the late autumn, redwings and fieldfares roost in the trees and it is possible to see merlin, hen harriers and the odd peregrine on the wing with woodcock and snipe rising from the boggy depressions. The cries of the thrushes lend a poignancy to this silent resting place of the tin industry. Then the Hawk training aircraft come roaring low over the moor and the peace is shattered. This age is a loud one and even on Dartmoor it is impossible to escape entirely the implications of science and technology and noise pollution. In the jet fighters mineral has been elevated to a frightening art form. They appear from nowhere on a burst of noise that fuses the nerves in ones fingertips and dumps one right back in the twentieth century.

Tom Endacott's farmyard, Creaber, Gidleigh.

JOURNEYS

At dawn the weather was fine. There were patches of blue sky over the moors and the air was warm. I walked up the West Dart until I crossed the river and climbed the slopes of Beardown. A buzzard flapped away, keeping low. Maybe it had killed and was unwilling to abandon its prize.

I walked on. It was cooler now and thunder growled across from Bellever and the east, followed by a louder peal. Over Higher White Tor sheet lightning lit the horizon. Gradually the thunder became a regular din and, shortly after I arrived at Lydford Tor, it began to rain. Big heavy drops beat against my cagoule and slammed into my legs. The thunder crashed and a series of tremendous explosions jolted through the deepening gloom. The downpour became a cold deluge but I was unwilling to shelter among the rocks as forked lightning flickered against the murk. The electricity in the atmosphere was lifting my hair.

Between the boom and crack of the thunder and its slow rumble away into short-lived silence, the lightning struck and I wondered if any of the bolts crackling down uncomfortably close had my name on them.

I left the high ground and marched briskly back towards Two Bridges along the Devonport Leat. Sheep and cattle seemed remarkably unconcerned by the noise and the livid flares in the sky. By the time the hotel was reached my legs were soaked and water was sloshing around in my boots. The storm raged as I sat and drank coffee and thought of other Dartmoor autumn spectaculars. A group of pony mares and foals trotted across the road and wandered down to the riverside. The lightning lent a theatrical garishness to the trees and grass; but the moor was still the best place on earth and the rain-soaked landscape smelt of wet stone and water and leaves ground to a brown mash by passing cars.

Returning the following day I saw the red flag flying from the pole on Beardown Tors. They were firing on the Okehampton Range and the Merrivale Field Firing Area was also in use. I had forgotten to ring one of the telephone numbers listed on the North Sheet of the Ordnance Survey map of Dartmoor 28 to tap the answering services which give information about firing times. The Danger Area marked on the map is vast. It accounts for most of the North Moor and I confess to being irritated on occasions by the military presence, by the little green huts on rocks like Rough Tor and Great Mis Tor. The armed forces are clamouring for more wilderness, yet the great deserted spread of high ground owes its solitude to yet another paradox in human nature. The military's constant need to practice the killing skills guarantees the existence of the place as a real wildlife reserve. Young soldiers train there and will continue to do so for as long as fear and suspicion prevail among nations. What may be bad news for humanity tomorrow is good news for wildlife today; but the irony leaves me cold.

On the ranges preparation for war is working unwittingly on behalf of other creatures, and the great spaciousness from Okehampton in the north to Fernworthy Forest in the east, Beardown in the south and Willsworthy Artillery Range to the west is a vast unofficial sanctuary. In the current political climate, muscle must apparently be flexed; but when the red flags fly and the shells fly and the small arms chatter, the birds continue to sing and the fox lies on his couch of heather ignorant of all the human confusion around him.

Yet it is wonderful to meet a young couple on some remote hill or a family coming off high ground after a day spent close to Nature. Such encounters at Wistman's Wood are common but the area around the copse is never crowded. Go there on an autumn weekday and that part of the West Dart will almost certainly be deserted. The sparkle of a morning drowned in golden light, with nothing but larksong and river sounds lapping at the hush, can make the visit to the wood itself seem incidental. To breathe the cool autumn air among the tors under a blue sky is to know a great happiness.

I can recall hunting that happiness as a boy, when the wilderness gave me everything. I ran through it and was part of it and fed it and fed on it and believed the spirit of the place was all life.

The gnarled and stunted oaks rooted between boulders in Wistman's Wood.

Wistman's Wood is there on the lower eastern slopes below the ridge which culminates in Longaford Tor. The mass of pale brown and bronze foliage does not look like a stand of trees and when you reach it you understand why. The gnarled and stunted oaks are rooted between the boulders of a long clitter, covering an area of about four acres. The deep pockets of humus offer root purchase and shelter from the wind to trees whose twisted branches have entwined in their creep across the rocks. The trunks and boughs are covered in lichens and mosses, and epiphytic ferns also sprout from the bark. Wherever there is a precarious hold there is plant life.

Among the mature oaks, some of which may be four hundred years old, is the odd rowan. A few small birds are in residence but woodrush and whortleberry flourish here and so does myth. The devil and his Wish or Whist hounds are said to lie up under the dwarf oaks between sorties to hunt human souls. A glimpse of the huge black dogs with their eyes like red hot coals means death within the year or a brief run before the slavering jaws into cardiac arrest or a nastier conclusion. All I've ever found in the wood is peace and beauty; and one spring just after Hitler's War I looked down from the Devonport Leat and saw a vixen and her cubs leave the clitter to play in the sun. If you meet the devil there or anywhere else on the moors you brought him with you.

The road from Two Bridges east to Postbridge, which I usually take after a morning at Wistman's or a day on the mires around Fur Tor, is part of the mediaevel packhorse route that linked Plymouth and Moretonhampstead. Postbridge has a hospitable pub, a stonewaller and a farm where champion sheepdogs are bred. It is a beauty spot with a funny little post office stores and a superb clapper bridge. In former times packhorse teams carrying tin and other goods crossed the East Dart, walking safely over this bulky structure of moorstone slabs, which is supported by buttresses and piers of granite. Smaller clapper bridges can be seen elsewhere on the moors occasionally as parts of the ancient tracks which crossed rivers as they threaded between communities and places or offered routes over potentially dangerous coun- try. The hazards of the mediaeval wilderness were many – robbers, blizzards, fog and flooding; but the high moor was traversed by a variety of travellers from tinkers to pilgrims and even corpses.

The Lichway or Way of the Dead runs from the eastern side of the moor to Lydford in the west, although many of its former users would have been unaware of the long journey, twelve miles as the crow flies. As the mediaeval forest was in Lydford parish, the people living there had to visit the church for a number of reasons including baptisms, weddings and funerals. Apart from its ecclesiastical status, Lydford was also the centre of law and order with its courts and gaol. Enforced journeys to the place in bad weather must have been nightmarish especially for the unfortunates carrying heavy coffins from beyond the East Dart. All burials had to take place at Lydford and bearers, working alternately in teams, would have marched slowly along the track, fording the rivers and skirting the mires as they came over the Cowsic and Walkham, across Peter Tavy Great Common and Willsworthy to journey's end. The wilderness can have held few attractions for those men.

From 1260 the ancient tenements of Babeny and Pizwell on the East Dart were allowed to bury their dead at Widecombe Church, much closer to home. Near the roadside on the hill south east of Dartmeet, the Coffin Stone is a reminder of those funeral processions. The stone itself is split in two, supposedly by a bolt of lightning from Heaven which struck the coffin containing an evil man. Box and corpse went up in flames and the stone was left as it is today.

Farmer Jack Powlesland of Throwleigh with hook and stone.

THE DRIFTS AND BEYOND

At times it is like stepping into the living poetry of Genesis. A wild place, water and rock, horizons uncluttered by buildings – all conspire to create a compelling mystery. Yet it may be an illusion. On the open moor, like practically everywhere else on earth, man and Nature meet on human terms and somewhere along the line 'romance' is eclipsed by pounds, shillings and pence.

Many of us see moorland forestry as the geometry of greed. The map has far too many of those sinister green blocks, marked 'Plantation' representing mainly Forestry Commission conifers. To come upon close-packed regiments of trees in the open wilderness is depressing. They are an intrusive farm crop, another of those blunt 'economic realities' Big Business can get away with. The firs bring the flowing lines of the landscape to an abrupt end and nearly every reservoir has its ranks of dull money-making trees.

Massive planting operations led to the vandalising of Fernworthy, Bellever and Laughter Hole. In a few decades the wilderness landscape was seriously threatened by afforestation. Then, in 1951, Dartmoor became a National Park and although the Park Authority's power was limited, it deployed a shrewd diplomacy. During the early Fifties, the Forestry Commission was talked out of planting on Haytor Down of all places, arguably one of the most beautiful stretches of the moor. But the growth of private forestry with its considerable government backing is sure to create problems and the planting of sensitive areas will almost certainly occur unless the timber growers are subjected to planning control. Greedy landowners should not be given the freedom of the moors while the small farmer struggles against the odds to make his holding pay and the public out walking find their way blocked by plantations.

In the early days trees were planted around the reservoirs in the belief that they would attract clouds to ensure an almost continual supply of rain. It was one of those quaint notions worthy of great Victorian eccentrics. At Burrator Reservoir random summer-leafing trees like the beech confer an Englishness on the scene which the tightly packed masses of 'Christmas trees' cannot impair. Burrator, surrounded by the cool browns, buffs and washed-out yellows of the hills, is considered to be a jewel among the moor's reservoirs. Beeches flaming from the larches and less compromising firs lend seasonal loveliness to the waterside. If trees have to be stuck around the artificial lakes – Burrator, Venford, Kennick, Fernworthy, Meldon and Avon – why not silver birch, rowan, beech and hawthorn? Better still, when the present stands of firs are felled why not let the vegetation return exactly as it chooses?

In the autumn the surface of Burrator mirrors the sky's gold and the shores are strewn with beech leaves. The low-flying aircraft do not cause a flutter among the rafts of wildfowl and the snarling whine of a chainsaw goes unnoticed by birds and animals. Sunlight penetrates the conifer gloom and beauty exists in the most unlikely places. The darkest plantation is capable of presenting the happy surprise of antiquity preserved in a stone circle or the fleet departure of a roebuck. But viewed from a distance across the open moor, the green patches suggest a mercenary human vision which, if it is permitted to expand, will mean the end of the wilderness.

Hill farming is very much a part of the Dartmoor fabric. It is rooted in antiquity and the grazing animals are the farmers' basic livelihood. For the visitor the moors may be full of mystery, clad in beauty or frightening bleakness. For farmstock it is grim reality. It is obvious that certain aspects of this husbandry have become un-acceptable – morally, anyway. The pony, for instance, is often exploited as if it has no intrinsic right to an existence free from pain and suffering. The roadside tourists, who believe these animals to be wild, are unaware of the implications of autumn in pony terms. October is a mellow time, but the mares and foals may be more plump from red worm than from the summer grazing. On the hills all around them sheep and cattle are looking good for market. Nights are ablaze with the huge bright stars of the season. The souvenir shops and cafes are closed, the pubs are quiet and the Devon accent surfaces to muzz the whist drives. Across the side of the downs the pony herds chest the bracken. The animals are at peace with themselves.

Then, from the distance, comes the mounting snarl of a scrambler bike. The mares' ears prick and their heads turn towards the noise. Down the hillside sweeps a straggling half circle of men on horses and motorbikes. The ponies begin to run across the road and on among the stone rows. The men pursue them, shouting and whooping. There is the thunder of hooves and the awful insistent snarl of the Japanese motorbikes. The pony drift has begun. But after the initial panic the animals become almost manageable. Although they are harrassed, barked at by dogs and frightened by the machines and bigger horses, they allow themselves to be driven along the road towards the pub in the coombe. They run together, mares and foals, over the bridge to the pound where they are penned and sorted ready for the sales.

The autumn drifts bring the animals streaming down off the open moor for the fairs at Ashburton, Chagford and Tavistock. Once the ponies were profitable livestock, now they represent a bit of extra pocket money for the farmer's wife. Today's owner will be lucky to get thirty-five pounds for a mare and ten pounds for a foal. Consequently their status among farm animals is low and their lives brief and, for the most part, miserable.

The foals, most of which are uncut colts, have a life expectancy of six or seven months; some less. From the pound at the end of the drift, the animals are taken to the sale and the trauma of separation, mares from young.

Unable to reason, ponies like all animals have no knowledge of death. But they become agitated and bewildered in the holding pens where the demeanor of the men breeds tension, although the proceedings are watched over by RSPCA officers. Horses and ponies are less docile than sheep or cattle in stressful circumstances and the humans generate an atmosphere of agression.

At the sales the animals resist and have to be manhandled into the auction ring, and the onlooker will perhaps recognise something tragic and unsavoury about the way the creatures are brought under the hammer. It goes beyond townee sentimentality. These ponies are destined for the slaughterhouse. The mares will end up in French and Belgian restaurants; the foals will become petfood, on sale on super-

Tavistock pony sale.

market shelves all over Britain. The lucky few will be bought by Horse and Pony sanctuaries, like the one at Manaton, or by caring members of the public. The majority are sold to a small clique of men buying for the abbatoirs and are held in collecting pens with someone's name chalked on the gate.

Their heads droop, they pant, their flanks heave, they are acutely distressed, their lips are drawn back to show their teeth. The whinneying and neighing rising from the pens is the din of despair and bewilderment. It mingles with the bellowing and roaring of the men chivvying the animals in and out of the ring.

Finally they are herded up ramps into lorries, mares and foals in separate lots. Sometimes a foal slips and crashes onto its side. Then it is gripped by the mane and tail and flung back into the press of terrified animals. The RSPCA officers stand by and, although their presence has ended the real cruelty which occurred in the past, the foals in particular still suffer. And for what reason? Tradition? Economically their existence cannot be justified. On an overstocked moor they help reduce the grazing and it would be better for the ponies if most of them were replaced by a few more Galloways. At least that would end the sagas of neglect and ill treatment which begin at birth. Better they had not been born.

I'm glad there are survivors of the drifts and fairs but it is a pity that pony protection societies are necessary. When the stocks of ponies are reduced they should not be increased again to even the present level. Fewer animals would be manageable and, under a new policy, could enjoy a longer and happier lease of life. This is sane economics, not sentimentality. A good beef animal is worth a dozen ponies. Half a dozen herds of pure-bred Dartmoors running on lease over the National Park, managed by the Park Authority would create a realistic situation. The ponies would continue to be a tourist attraction and the farmers would get subsidies for keeping them. Then the drifts and the sales of frightened creatures would become things of the past and more grazing would be available for the sheep and cattle.

After the drifts the hills seem empty. The rowan and birch leaves continue to fall and scatter on the wind. The mist shifts in the valley with the tors rising above it as remote from earth as any mountain peaks. Then the top of Cox Tor can be an island in the sky. The mist thins and lies in bands between the hills. Whiteness has faded to grey in the Tamar Valley but to the north the white reefs remain. The sky is glazed with autumn's coolness. Three pony mares and two filly foals appear on the summit to crop what is left of the grass. The mist continues to drift away. The mares and their young have survived along with a few other lucky females throughout the moor to become the breeding stock of the future.

WINTER

GNARLED ROOTS SNAKE
INTO THE CHINKS AND CREVICES
BETWEEN THE STONES AND,
WHERE THE SNOW LIES ON AUTUMN'S LEAF-LITTER,
THERE IS THE WHISPERED MOVEMENT
OF WOOD MICE

Previous page: Annie Harvey plucking a fowl at Batworthy Farm.

WEATHER

The north east wind moaned through the ribs of the dead sheep on the upland where wild weather is born. The sky was full of snow and the wind was strong enough to uproot trees. I could lean against it.

Whenever I tugged at the side of my balaclava I let in the noise. The gloom rose to a roar and subsided again to a wavering, hollow whine. The morning opened before me and I was alone on the downs. Between snow flurries were glimpses of distances; but the white-scribbled wind only dropped briefly, like a flapping curtain. The cold filmed my eyes and made me aware of the shape of my nostrils. Whenever the roar abated light grew in the sky, but the gloom always won. Ahead, the horizon was darkening and I knew what it signified. My rucksack was crammed with survival gear and I had followed the mountain code to the letter.

The snow was already five or six inches deep and the wind was sculpting it into drifts and making the hilltops smoke. I came down off high ground into the valley and followed the stream. Birds had left their tracks on the whiteness and among them were the larger footprints of rabbits, hares and foxes.

The cold intensified in the copse of oaks and rowans, and the first hard grains of the blizzard were being blasted horizontally through the treetops. I crouched behind a bole and ate some mintcake and had a swig of coffee from the flask. The gritty flakes shot across the valley.

I walked up the cart track. In places the drifts were already three feet deep and visibility was down to ten yards. Snow was swirling out of a white void. I checked the compass although the track was familiar. It led onto open heather moor where the wind blew unchecked and the snow grains stung my face. The fallen snow creamed around my knees as I came onto the road south of the cattle grid. A small group of ponies walked ahead of me and vanished in the white-out. The blizzard flowed, ebbed and crashed in again. I stared into a blurred, noisy world. The wind was razor sharp and, whenever the fall of flakes dwindled to a handful, I could see the snow smoke billowing from the nearby tors.

For the experienced hill walker, who is well-prepared and knows the moors and his own limitations, winter is an exciting season. For a few months the remoter parts of the wilderness are left to themselves and coming to them alone is an adventure. But you have to work to earn that privilege. Fitness is essential if you want to clock the miles, and hillcraft is about learning all the time and acquiring experience.

There is always something going on in the grass and heather, the streams, rivers and sky. It hinges on using the eyes as they are rarely used in town. Looking up I am often astonished to find so much beauty above and around me. This spaciousness is a startling aspect of the moor's magic.

There have been times when I've thought that my life needed no other justification than a walk over snow hills, completely at peace with myself. What the landscape gave me I had found in childhood, never to mislay.

I have lost count of the occasions when I've climbed onto the Chinkwell and Honeybag Ridge after a blizzard had blanco'd the East Moor. The ascent of the steeps still makes me aware of the muscles in my legs and the joy of scrambling onto a high wild place. Throughout my boyhood I thought of the prehistoric hunters who must have sweated up the slopes in winter as I did.

The Ridge falls into space and it is possible to look east across the whiteness to the rocks of the Down and the great 'diamond' of Hay Tor commanding the landscape. The wind whines through stone walls and forces the grass haulms and heather stabs to sing. Light glints on ice and lifts brilliance from the snow crystals. Half blinded by the knife-blade glare it is a joy to discover yellow gorse flowers crisped within clear ice. Winter rain and fog have produced memorable occasions, although rain on Dartmoor is either there or never far away. Leaving the mire and the wellhead of two rivers I came down towards the farm and the road. A twelve bore banged and a pigeon fell from vivid life into darkness.

Drystone walls provide shelter at Whiteworks, with Foxtor Mire beyond.

At the sett by the tor, men had been digging for badgers. The tor was part of the rain in the sky that was falling. Behind the rain came the cold blue and the thunder-heads. Soon half the moor was being battered by hail. Rivers climbed their banks but the herons continued to stalk the floodwater and lapwings flung themselves about on the wind. Field corners became pools and ponies stood silently in their daydreams of hunger. Water beaded on wire and rock, feather, hair and beak. Farm workers and farm animals moved with a slow-motion plod.

Then the rain and hail passed and fog muffled the high places, holding them in a hush. Cold intensified and moisture settled as hoarfrost. Dusk sent the fox padding across the empty car park. Wings rushed overhead. The wind sighed in the grass and heather. Below the fog the in-country valley smelt of woodsmoke. Someone was sawing logs and great congregations of birds were coming in to roost. The empty crow's nest shook in the bare hawthorn tree and leafless rowans bent and swayed in the hedgerows.

But the new day can bring its surprises.

A bloodless sun was printed on the mist and the first cars of the morning swished along the moorland road. Sheep bleated, a crow rasped, water gurgled over stone. Then the hawk lifted from the heather-choked goyal near the top of the valley. It climbed swiftly on ash-grey wings with black-tipped pinions like fingers held slightly apart. Soon it was above me and flying away, but in the binocular window the grey of throat and breast fading into white was clearly visible. Then the male hen-harrier vanished into the mist leaving me alone below the warren.

The hen-harrier quartered the slopes during the short daylight hours of winter, when the landscape was apparently comatose. Unlike the buzzards they are silent birds, hunting low with a few beats of their wings and a glide and a pounce. Their prey varies from grouse and rabbits to smaller creatures like voles, songbirds, frogs and beetles. Their greyness is of the Dartmoor mists which wreathed the mine workings and the upper reaches of the river.

The Forestry Commission plantation below was invisible but the whisper of wings announced the departure of birds. I crouched in the heather while the mist around me vanished. Flocks of foreign thrushes were on the move. Usually birds are reluctant to fly when fog closes but, descending almost to the conifers, I found the valley clear and sunny. Returning to the road I entered the mist again but the whisper of wings followed me as I walked.

A week later the snow returned.

It fell from a relentless north-easter and drifted against hedges and walls. The grey, coppery-tinged sky was dark with the threat of blizzard. Beyond Okehampton Camp lay the winter wilderness as few visitors see it. The temperature was below zero and the massive drifts on the loop road were frozen so hard I could walk on them. To my right were West Mill Tor, Yes Tor and High Willhays. The gale force wind was lifting the snow and sending it streaming away in phantoms.

At the bridge over the Black-a-Ven Brook I found a downfall of ice and frozen bog. Keeping to the road I came into the tundra country by stormlight. Then I trekked to Yes Tor and High Willhays. The additional four hundred feet of altitude (the brook is around 1,600 feet above sea level and both tors are fractionally over 2,000 feet) lent an abrasiveness to the wind. The hood of my cagoule was vibrating as I stumbled and danced over the clitters to stand first on Yes Tor then High Willhays, which is the highest point on Dartmoor. The snow against the slate grey sky had a fantastic luminosity.

Courtney Mortimore and one of his sons feeding silage at Green Combe near Jurston.

LIVESTOCK

The snowplough pushing up the hill, where the road is narrow, shatters part of the drystone wall. A raven croaks and the raw wild cry of a peregrine carries across the stillness of a fresh snowfall. The surface powder fumes off the downs and the bitter cold and shortage of food begin to take their toll of the sheep and ponies. On the high moor the wind-ruffled bodies of mares reduced to skin and bone by the hardship of winter are not an uncommon sight. Crows scavenge the wastes. They winkle out the eyes of weak sheep that have fallen and the animals blunder around until death releases them. Sheep walk before the blizzard until they come up against a wall or a tor. Then the drifts cover them and some perish. Ponies and cattle walk into the wind, but the vast majority of cattle are brought down when the weather is bad.

Farming and overstocking can go hand in hand and winter feed is sometimes denied to the animals that most need it. Year after year ponies and sheep are caught on the open moor by atrocious weather.

The Dartmoor Livestock Protection Society has been campaigning for over twenty years in an attempt to persuade reluctant farmers to take animals from the high wilderness when snow warnings are issued.

The problem is as vast as the wilderness and the crows and foxes are never without a meal. But there is a hard core of caring livestock owners whose example should serve the entire Dartmoor agricultural community. They value and respect their animals, and their love of moorland life is expressed in hard work and dedication; and throughout the winter that life is hard although the people involved in it rarely complain.

My response to the wilderness is coloured by what I am and do and by my feelings for the landscape and nature, yet I am always the onlooker and although I come often to the moors my relationship with it lacks the farmer's intimacy. The world takes on a totally different perspective when your knuckles are cracking and bleeding with cold, and the wind has smacked the feeling out of your face. The penance of changing a tractor tyre in sub-zero temperatures or doing the daily chores in cold, driving rain produces a tough breed. Few townspeople could endure the life. In snow and ice the reality slams home. Animals have to be fed and cared for on the home pastures and further afield if their owner is operating efficiently and compassionately and wants his farm to survive.

Meanwhile the wind blows, the rain falls or the snow falls and the livestock demand attention. Winter on a Dartmoor hill farm is all expenditure. Everywhere he looks the farmer sees his overdraft on the hoof.

I came to the farm above the river valley in late January. A wind heavy with the promise of snow was roaring in the beech trees. The moors north of Princetown were white against a leaden sky that held a dull orange glow near the horizon. The farmyard was quiet. Fowls ranged over dung heaps and the piles of soiled bedding forked out of the byres. Every so often a horse or calf pushed its head from the window to round its nostrils and look at me. In the linhay two old ponies were asleep on their feet.

Then with a clank of pails and the sound of human voices, the farm came alive. The lady went from outhouse to outhouse with nuts, grain and hay, and I could hear the 'chomp' of feeding animals. Calves were tugging hay from the nets and rolling their jaws as they ate. Some of their companions drank noisily from the pails. Hooves clattered and grated on stone. Plumes of breath rose from the half-darkness and a strange little collie-cross on heat snarled at the Jack Russell whose attentions she did not welcome.

Again I was the onlooker and again I could not ignore the beauty of the place and the occasion. The byre smelt of animals and animal living, and the gentle passiveness of the livestock reached out to me. Every day the cattle, ponies and sheep on this farm have their waiting period when they stand motionless in cowhouse or field or in groups on the open moor. Perhaps an ear will twitch or their eyes will

Middlecot Farm near Chagford.

Right: Dr Duncan Fraser examining
a pregnant mare at Moor Gate.
Above: Smallholder Peter Hannaford
of Higher Sherwell.

widen and pick up something in particular – a bird in the sky, a tree swaying in the wind. Then all of a sudden the tractor comes reeling and rocking and bumping up the lane with their feed and they are instantly alert. They break ranks and follow at a steady pace until that pace quickens and they are running after the tractor. Each of them is fully alive again and all that anticipation has paid off. Bales of hay are tossed from the trailer and broken up to a lowing chorus or happy bleating.

When the weather is rough and a bitter wind is blowing you sometimes find farm animals waiting beside the road or in field corners for the tractors to come. Like all grazing creatures they live within their gentleness and unhurriedly turn their heads and swing their gaze at you.

In the winter the two distinct faces of moorland farming are most apparent. Neglect, with the sheep and ponies left in terrible conditions to fend for themselves, litters the wilderness with bones. Of the holdings which care for their stock and give it every consideration, to say the animals are loved would not be far-fetched. Yet the good farmer does not dramatise his circumstances, especially if he works on a small farm. Grass runs out about Christmas and he and his family tackle the maintenance jobs – the walling and ditching – before the animals have regularly to be fed.

Feeding goes on until the spring and fresh growth. The cows get their feed until the beginning of May when most have calved. The best part of the farmer's working day, six or seven hours, is spent feeding his stock. For them the freedom of a hard life which isn't bound to time is the attraction, but they recognise that the life-style is changing. Few youngsters want to ride a horse when they can leap onto a motorbike. Change manifests itself in many ways. Buying-in forage in the winter with the price of hay constantly going up and meat prices dropping must be depressing. Diesel is also costly. Yet, despite the setbacks, the caring farmer remains attached to his animals and even aged cows and horses are not parted with easily.

SHADOWS ON THE SNOW

For most of us the moor is synonymous with freedom – the freedom to walk for miles away from the cares of everyday life. For others 'The Moor' has a sinister ring. It's another name for Dartmoor Prison and few prisons in Europe have bleaker locations.

The inside is claustrophobia made concrete, a world of locks, keys, suspicion and routine, and minds obsessed by time.

During winter especially, the surrounding wilderness is an extension of the place, and looking up at the Latin words inscribed over the main gateway one wonders at the sentiment which inspired them: *Parcere Subjectis* – 'Spare the humbled'.

There is much of the surrealistic about those grey buildings in the snow in the middle of an arctic waste. Behind the iced-wire is a self-contained community of men put in quarantine by the rest of society. Beyond one wall is another and, between them, prison officers with their dogs patrol night and day. The numbers on the walls are important. In the event of a breakout the officer can call for assistance on his radio, pinpointing the exact spot by the figures on the stonework. The third wall is the moor itself, and perhaps winter is yet another barrier.

Behind the walls and rolled razor wire are the cell blocks with their barred windows, the nissen-style buildings and the exercise yard. The interior of the massive granite cellblocks is functional to the extreme: galleries, the single cells, netting between landings and metal stairs. Endlessly throughout the day, men are mopping up or soaping down the place, while others sew mailbags or lie on their beds in the cells. The inmates have to be kept occupied as they live between meals and the exercise yard, with time carrying them towards freedom as slowly as a glacier. Here human lives have been deposited in the deep freeze.

Iced trees stir above the sheet ice on heather and the iced gorse spines. There are jewel trees standing in jewel grass against sun-gold bracken. This is a landscape designed to foster hyperbole. The beauty is soul-piercing and one image leads to

Dartmoor Prison, Princetown.

another: organ-pipe icicles on the banks of a frozen stream; snow flowing over the surface of the moor; stormy skies and tors heaving out of freezing fog; jackdaws printed on whiteness; flocks of chaffinches like Christmas decorations on bare trees. Horses and cattle seek the lee of walls as the north-east wind cuts across the countryside. It is a wind that kills but it can also clothe the trees in loveliness.

Close to most human habitation on the moors are beeches, often in tall stately hedges growing out of stone walls. Like the trees around a farm these hedges provide shelter for animals. Standing, ice-plastered or holding the sun-dapple on the grey 'rind' of their bark, they are also expressions of the miraculous. Gnarled roots snake into the chinks and crevices between the stones and, where the snow lies on autumn's leaf-litter, there is the whispered movement of wood mice.

Beeches have a majesty which rowans cannot match but how impoverished Dartmoor would be without this most celtic of British trees. Mountain ash is an apt name for the graceful little tree but I prefer the name rowan. Our ancestors planted them near their houses to keep away evil spirits. Coming down off the high moor it is always good to chance on one growing in the rock clitter beside a stream. For me they represent the spirit of Dartmoor. The hawthorn possesses a similar toughness and tenacity. With winter hard set, the clusters of wine-dark berries on spiky twigs attract the fieldfares and redwings.

Hawthorns were once planted on banks throughout Britain – as boundary markers. They surpass the blackthorn in beauty although I remain in love with blackthorn blossom which for me is the finest prelude to spring the Westcountry can lift from winter's stranglehold.

At Burrator Reservoir there is ice on the trees and the water. Among the conifers are siskins and crossbills eating the seeds of the cones, while under the beeches flocks of chaffinches work through the drifts of mast for autumn leftovers. Out on the lake are mallard, pochard and teal, with rafts of goosanders congregating after the evening flight. When the blizzards blow wild swans also splash down onto the water and tufted duck and golden eye are regular visitors. The cries of siskins and crossbills on a frosty morning after snow and wildfowl calling across a flat calm make Burrator delightful during the hard uncompromising months.

Yet reminders of the tourist season surface from the landscape. A few gnomes, some wrapped up against the damaging cold, stand or lie in the snow outside the pixie centre. The tourist 'honeypots' are dead and a scattering of ponies walk the deserted roads of Widecombe whose community life is centred on the Church of Saint Pancras. The fine granite tower, that features on so many Westcountry calendars, adds to the grandeur of a winter day. Little wonder the church is also known as the Cathedral of the Moor.

THE GOOD LADIES

The windswept hills were speckled with snow. It was a cold day and the foxhunt had met at Cold East Cross. Foot followers gathered at Hemsworthy Gate and discussed the proceedings. Blackslade Down had proved a blank but later as I walked Haytor Down I saw the pack streaming down Houndtor Valley giving tongue. The hounds ran along the flanks of Holwell with the 'field' hopelessly adrift behind them. Then they checked.

From the top of Smallacombe Rocks the drama unfolded. On every side the piebald moor swam away to the sky and the belling of the pack carried for miles. Bands of riders drove their horses across the hillside, but the hounds were noisily descending the public footpath under Greator Rocks to disappear in the larch plantation. Their baying rang through the valley. Somewhere the fox was running for its life.

At Hound Tor I met the icy wind again. The hunt had gone on beyond Great Hound Tor, but the faint clamour of the pack was still audible. Occasionally I met foot followers but that was the last I saw of the hounds or the horsemen that day.

Towards the end of winter the meet was at the pub by the bridge. It was a cheerful gathering. Stirrup cups were handed around. The hounds were whining. People sat on their horses chattering and laughing.

Eventually the hunt moved off down the road and over the ridge. Soon red coats could be seen in the pasture among the sheep. Before long the fox appeared on the skyline – then the hounds. The fox came down the hill into cover. A line of riders galloped along the ridge and the hounds came crashing into the valley through the bracken. Later the fox went to ground and the huntsman dismounted and walked over to the bank and waited for the terrier man and his animals. Men were looking down holes but the fox bolted and, although the hounds took off in pursuit, it was lost.

When the arctic spell persisted they held a foot hunt, mainly to keep the hounds in trim. These powerful black and tan animals with their intelligent noses, sloping shoulders, straight legs, stamina, speed and endurance are handsome creatures. Their existence is generally short, happy and exciting and very few live to be old. A hound incapable of working with the pack is destroyed.

Watching them range over the snowscape attended by the master and the huntsman and a few dedicated followers, I became aware of the hugeness of the moor. Tiny figures climbed a white hillside. A woman pointed to the fox's hiding place. The hounds cast about but cold stifles scent and their chances of finding were remote.

The walkers and the animals made their way to the crest of the hill, but the master remained on the slopes with a solitary hound. Landrovers and hunt followers were on the narrow road. Birds were flocking and then the hounds were among the trees, running out of sight.

At length they were there on the immense snowscape and so far off they were as small as ants. The master's horn yelped across the wind-ruffled hush. It was a beautiful, bleak sound.

Four packs hunt Dartmoor where there are a lot of foxes. The fox is the great opportunist. Some kill lambs; most eat carrion and a wide range of other food from blackberries and dung beetles to voles, mushrooms and rabbits. The farming community demands they are kept down and foxes are shot and trapped as well as hunted to death. The kills by the hunt, which I have witnessed over the years, have been swift. A hound considerably outweighs a fox. It goes for the neck and the cervical vertebra and as the fox's central nervous system fails the creature dies. Some kills are slower.

Most hunting folk genuinely ride to hounds for the exhilaration of the gallop and the thrill of being in the saddle in a wild place on a good day. But at the end of the chase there is the kill.

The claim that rural economy would be hard hit if fox hunting were banned by law appears to be unfounded. Drag hunting is an obvious alternative. This would keep the saddlemaker and the farrier and everyone else involved in the business employed, and ensure the survival of the hounds. Then the 'picturesque' side of the hunt – the red coats, the scrum of tail-wagging hounds, the stirrup cups, hard riding across open country and the music of the horn – would excite no criticism or protest.

Hunt advocates claim that the abolition of hunting would ring the death knell for the English fox as a species. They insist that widespread persecution through trapping, gassing, poisoning and shooting would lead to its extinction. Could such a campaign be justified? Well, the urban fox has proved no great pest despite the rumours about its taste for cats! Would the wilderness population increase to an alarming extent if numbers were not kept down?

At one time foxes had to be imported from the continent to provide the hunts with their sport; and during the war when hunting was postponed for five or six years there was no population explosion. But today the fox is tolerated by many farmers because of the hunt. Without the hunt would the shooting, trapping, poisoning and gassing lead to much greater suffering and a drastic reduction in numbers?

Compared to the fox, the badger has been subjected to unbelievable cruelty for centuries, yet it is among the moor's most beautiful residents. Even on a bad day the animals are active and their footprints in the snow put an end to the untruth of winter hibernation. The sow has her young in February, although they won't come above ground for about six or eight weeks. The creature is now at her most vulnerable to the predation of the badger diggers or The Ministry of Agriculture.

The war waged on all sides against the animals has forced a handful of dedicated people to mount guard over the setts or to create sanctuaries. The diggers unearth the badger and either kill it on the spot or carry it off to the blood rituals of the baiting. It is easily done. Men with terriers go to the sett and check for signs that it is occupied. Maybe fresh dung in the latrine pits or fresh grass and bracken bedding in the holes are sufficient to get them working. The Jack Russell is put into the sett and investigates the tunnels and chambers until the badgers are located. Its muffled barking tells the men above where to dig. Picks, spades and bars open the ground and the heavy, long-handled badger tongs clamp to the animal. The iron bites into hide, flesh and muscle and the badger is dragged out to be beaten to death or removed to somewhere

Headland Warren Farm in a landscape shaped by tin mining.

Left: Reaves beneath Corndon Tor.
Above: The enamelled beauty of an ice-coated landscape.

Powder Mills Farm near Postbridge, beneath Longaford Tor.

quiet and private for the baiting. Then fighting dogs, like the Staffordshire Bull Terriers, are unleashed and literally worry the animal to the point of death in a way which has given the word 'badgering' to the language.

During the ceaseless attacks, dogs as well as badgers are maimed or die. But for the sow or boar badger there is no escape. The men bet on the performance of their dogs or how long the victim will last. The coup de grace is administered with a blow from an iron bar or a spade if the animal survives the prolonged mauling.

Despite the vigilance of the protection groups, badgers are still being dug out of Dartmoor setts; but nationwide protest would produce the tough courtroom sentences diggers and baiters deserve. The barbarous activities of these men are a further diminishment of the wilderness moor. Yet the taking of badgers for 'sport' or any other reason is an offence under The Badger Protection Act of 1973 and The Wildlife and Countryside Act of 1981. An amendment in 1985 strengthened the Act – making it more difficult for the diggers to claim, if caught, they were after foxes.

The over-stretched resources of the RSPCA in general and the efforts of groups like the Dartmoor Badgers' Protection League and the Plymouth RSPCA Wildlife Group in particular, are obviously restricted by the size of the problem and geographical considerations. Organised gangs of badger baiters operate out of places like Plymouth and catching them in the act is difficult.

Among the methods they employ is lamping. Powerful lights are used to dazzle the badger, which is then netted for baiting sessions. Lurchers are sometimes used to turn the badgers into the nets. Under The Wildlife and Countryside Act, offenders could be fined the maximum £2,000, but even this does not discourage the unscrupulous. In the world of the baiter, terriers change hands for large sums of money and some court cases can create lucrative notoriety.

The deaths caused by the 'sportsmen' are dwarfed by the Ministry of Agriculture's activities. Mrs Brenda Charlesworth of the Dartmoor Badgers' Protection League claims that: 'Over the past ten years some 25,000 badgers have been put to death by the Ministry of Agriculture, despite the fact that they are legally protected animals.'

The Ministry's assertion that badgers give cattle Bovine Tuberculosis is, to say the least, controversial. Public pressure ended the wholesale gassing of badgers by the Ministry. Now the animals are live-trapped and shot and the death toll continues.

I met members of the Dartmoor Badgers' Protection League at a large sett above a river valley. Three or four young men stood about with their hands in their pockets as the snow fell in a slow drizzle. It was bitterly cold when Brenda Charlesworth appeared, but the weather did not bother this elderly lady. She wiped the snow off her glasses and stared across the moor. The sett had not been interfered with; but there were others to visit.

Mrs Charlesworth is the driving force behind the Poundsgate-based group and her home is usually full of League members preparing to go out on patrol in force, either to sabotage the Ministry of Agriculture's work or to confront the diggers.

Jill Hunt of the Plymouth RSPCA Rescue Group has a similar strong motivation. The Rescue Group concentrates entirely on wild animals and covers Plymouth, South Devon and Dartmoor. Jill speaks of setts which are dug time and time again. These are constantly inspected by the group. Members drive around day and night, usually in pairs. Using two-way radios they sometimes work with the police, especially after a strong tip-off when a sett may even be 'bugged'.

Diggers do get caught and punished; but the majority avoid detection and continue to dispense misery in pursuit of their 'sport'. Badger digging on Dartmoor is more difficult than it used to be, but the gangs still manage to leave the mutilated bodies of their victims at some of the setts like triumphant gestures.

Ruth Murray's Badger Sanctuary at Laughter Hole, Postbridge, is a haven for this beleagured species. Ruth is a tough, outspoken lady with strong views on protection. Her knowledge of badgers is vast and her reputation international. Laughter Hole is the result of a lifelong involvement with the mammal. Like the two other women at the forefront of the battle to free the badger from persecution, her commitment is total. Sickened by the sadism of the baiting gangs and the Ministry of Agriculture's wholesale slaughter policy, she created her sanctuary which people visit from all over the world, although it isn't open to the public. It is a quiet place among the pine trees of Bellever Forest. Yet the diggers penetrated on one occasion almost to her doorstep when they dug the sett at Laughter Tor. Ruth wasn't surprised. Badgers have been persecuted for hundreds of years.

Laughter Hole is many things – a permanent residence for some of the animals, temporary kennels for others, a refugee camp, study centre and 'convalescent home'. Animals turn up at the sanctuary for any number of reasons: as road-accident casualties, snare victims, digging victims and potential Ministry of Agriculture victims. They are also taken under Nature Conservancy Council licences, when there is a land development problem, such as a road going through a sett. Animals which survive the destruction of a sett cannot be released back into the same area and become lodgers until translocation is possible. The Ministry of Agriculture's current policy on Bovine TB outlaws such moves, which they claim could spread the disease, so some of the lodgers become residents.

Ruth Murray's philosophy is straightforward. Some animal welfare people reject the idea of keeping badgers penned but she believes life at Laughter Hole is preferable to a life of persecution and misery. If badger baiting were consigned to the history book along with bull-baiting and cock fighting and the Ministry of Agriculture halted its slaughter, there might be no need for sanctuaries and wildlife protection 'flying squads'.

But the wilderness continues to provide for its creatures. Watching the badger emerging from a sett on a starlit winter's night, swinging its black and white striped head as it analyses the wind, I cannot imagine anyone wanting to kill it. Carrying her grey bulk on short powerful legs the sow leaves the sett in the bank where the last field of the in-country farm meets the downs and trots off to forage. Below ground she has three cubs. Coming to a halt she lifts her muzzle but the night is free of man's taint and a moment later she bustles on. Behind her the snow smoke rises and whispers along the hillside.

AMMIL, MIRES AND WAYS

Much of Dartmoor is between a thousand and two thousand feet above the sea. The rounded hills offer little resistance to the winter winds that whistle down from Siberia. Despite its gentle appearance, the terrain is capable of blizzards so violent they have become part of folk history. For those who lived through it, the winter of 1947 is fresh in the mind. It was a sort of biblical disaster ending in the 'Great Ammil'. Snow fell ceaselessly for days on end, piling up rooftop-high and blocking the roads and railways. Reservoirs and streams froze and the animals caught in the open were buried where they stood. Communities were cut off and villages and farms were without bread and milk. The moors became a vast graveyard, packed with the carcasses of sheep, ponies and cattle. Canonteign Falls and Becky Falls were solid and the waterfall at Lydford Gorge was another great downfall of ice. In the bottom of a leaden sky the tors were icebergs. Even the rabbits were dying of starvation and foxes were seen rooting under the snow on farmland after the cabbages. The ice sheeting Leighon Ponds was littered with the bodies of redwings and fieldfares. Thousands of songbirds perished. Blizzards passed and were succeeded by other blizzards, and trees and telegraph poles crashed down. Then it began to drizzle.

The temperature was well below zero and the fine rain froze on contact with everything it touched. Presently the wind came strong from the north-west, turning the drizzle into an ice storm. At first the verglas formed on the windward side of twigs, grasses, wire, reeds, rocks and branches but when the storm died the drizzle fell steadily in a dense fog, covering the entire moor. Twigs swelled to five times their normal circumference and blackthorn trees became heavy 'cut-glass' sculptures. Branches were torn off by the weight of the ice; birches, rowans and beeches were brought down and telephone wires snapped. Reeds of ice stood beside stiff streams and the snowfields ran sparkling to ice-glazed tors.

All night and for most of the next day the moors were coated with frosted ice which Devonians called the 'ammil'. The lethal beauty has never been surpassed. Dartmoor looked as if it had been enamelled.

High places under snow and ice make wilderness-walking seductive; and I have crossed some of the worst mires when they have been frozen. Featherbed bogs which are normally small hollows full of vivid green sphagnum are never a problem. A plunge into one of them can result in nothing worse than wet feet. The blanket bogs of the North and South Moor are a different proposition and certain places on the South Moor, in particular, should be approached cautiously by walkers.

The Northern Mire of peat sog which can cover growan or rotted granite gives birth to five rivers. This bog is a desolate upland of cotton grass, moss and rushes, peat hags and water-filled channels.

The Rivers Avon, Plym, Swincombe and Erme begin on the other great blanket bog on the South Moor. Here, not far from Whiteworks, is the only really dangerous bog in the National Park, and it should always be treated with maximum respect. This is the notorious Fox Tor Mire which Conan Doyle re-christened Great Grimpen Mire in his Sherlock Holmes adventure, *The Hound of the Baskervilles.* People are said to have died here, swallowed by the peat gruel after going through the surface vegetation. I confess to a slight looseness of the bowels when I traversed it!

Three miles to the south east is Red Lake Mire which can be reached easily along the old dismantled tramway south of the China Clay Works at Redlake. Its surface yields alarmingly. A friend and I walked it one winter but even with the surface holding firm in the cold, the experience wasn't pleasant. Crossing the average valley bog is more interesting than perilous, but again wet socks are inevitable.

I usually associate wet feet with those seepage bogs which can be found on most hillsides above a coombe and a stream. To blunder into one of these in January or February, when the feet are freezing, can provoke colourful language. Experiences like this encourage careful route finding and map reading!

Even some of the mediaeval routes regularly taken by travellers in the old days are difficult to follow now, and in the winter the Abbot's Way on the South Moor can

become a puzzle. It is supposed to have been the chief monastic thoroughfare between the abbeys of Buckfast, Tavistock and Buckland. Tradition has it that Dartmoor's mediaeval crosses were erected by monks as guide stones for their 'paths', and they do stand on important routes; but some, such as Nun's Cross (or Siward's Cross) and Smalacumba Cross, served as boundary markers and this may have been the cross' original function. The Way is marked on The Ordnance Survey Map as passing from Buckfast Abbey to Nun's Cross, which is the halfway point, via Huntingdon Cross on the River Avon. If there were such a route, the placing of the crosses suggests it was more likely via Holne.

Towards the end of the Abbot's Way, Windy Post and Warren's Cross are worth a visit. Over the moor Huntingdon Cross, put there in the mid-16th century, is a nice piece of weathered granite. Touch it and you have living history beneath your fingertips.

After the blizzard was spent, the sky cleared and the sun came out. The hills were white silence. I walked into them as the buzzard idled across the late afternoon and began to circle. It explored the horizon in broad sweeps while I took in the smell of the landscape.

Light continued to fade and into the gathering dusk the buzzard descended to snuff out a small life. Violence is the Esperanto of raptors. Hawks and falcons kill quickly and soon the scattered fur or feathers and the bones become part of the winter landscape.

The Dartmoor dusk set the seal on a good day's walking. Tones deepened, snow brightness blued to lovely pallor, farm animals became featureless ghosts. Collecting my thoughts I saw the stars in the snow crystals and the sky.

Previous pages: **Road to Whiteworks, near Princetown, overlooking Foxtor Mire.**

SURVIVAL

Big fish were taking the weir at Buckfast Abbey. It was the morning of February 1st and the opening of the salmon fishing season. Along the Dart anglers were offering spinners to the heavy fish making their way upstream. Solway zippers, tweed hats and green thigh boots were visible among the trees. The river flowed full and clear and a thin sleet gusted from a wind that nettled the nose and ears.

For over twelve weeks of the close season the addicts had fretted and dreamed, lusting after the game fish, and that day a select few had congregated from all over Britain in the grey light of a Dartmoor morning. They had paid a lot of money to stand in the cold and cast a line, but beneath their passion for the sport was a deep love of the countryside. Being there really was enough and the sight of the leaping fish was obviously a tremendous bonus. To catch one with stealth and skill would have enhanced the occasion; but none were taken although they were the focal point of the anglers' morning.

The man fishing just below the weir was joined by a friend with three Jack Russells. The thunder of the water drowned all other sounds. Another angler and his labrador were further along the bank. Fish broke from the torrent and leapt. But the trees, the salmon, the sleet and the river provided something essential to the men on the banks. They spoke about the 'innocent' fish swimming against the current, the creatures that had not learnt guile. The salmon, which would come up later, would receive 'knowledge' of the impending danger when they detected a chemical solution secreted by frightened fish that had fought the hook or witnessed a life and death struggle. Beyond the conversations the salmon ran upstream to meet the challenge of the weir and race on like stabs of light underwater.

The sleet turned to snow which fell in big flakes. I left the Dart and memory deposited me onto another part of the moor in another winter. Rivers keep the past alive in the imagination. They rise and fall, roar or murmur, yet perpetually flow on the periphery of time; and one of my 'intimations of immortality' as a child was a Dartmoor stream.

Near the end of January 1986 I was down in a corner of the South West Moor after a thaw had begun with heavy rain and fog. The River Tavy cut through rough pasture and heath. Snowdrifts still clogged the lanes, and between the drifts the stony surface was ankle-deep in water. Rain slanted across the cries of lapwings. A fortnight of frost and a wind, like broken glass on the face, had been unkind to those birds. The country that normally provides insects and life had been hardened and some of the lapwings had died of starvation. But most had fled to the estuaries.

The rain lashed down but its noise was lost in the thunder of the river. The Tavy in spate was a force that claimed wildlife and farmstock. Meltwater surged in huge dirty brown waves which spilt over the banks on their race down to the Tamar.

The lapwings were crying a few days later when the snow returned, and as the sky darkened people spoke of the 1947 winter, wondering if they were in for something similar. Terrible winds swept across the moors and the snowfalls left behind them an eerie white and grey loveliness. Farm animals continued to die and the north-east wind showed no sign of slackening. It 'burnt' the gorse and heather and sent the snow swishing off the frozen surface of the roads. Walls vanished under drifts which were coated with frost and helicopters chuttered across the hills between squalls. It was another of those changeless aspects of the winter moors – the hardship of the hill flocks, the cruel beauty, the efforts of the caring.

Between blizzards I managed to walk from Leedon Tor to Ingra Tor and back – choosing this short route because the weather forecast promised another heavy snowfall later in the day.

Anyone who thinks the South West of England is soft, should stand on high Dartmoor in a black nor'easter in February. For all its soft curves this is 'Mountain Country', and it demands the respect the responsible hill walker gives to mountains in winter. To go onto the wilderness moor unprepared, alone or with equally unprepared friends, is to court disaster. When snow is on the ground and the sky is full of it, home is the best place to be and even on sunny, winter days I carry survival gear in my rucksack: compass, 'bivvy sack' (a strong plastic bag large enough to get inside if I'm be-nighted by a blizzard or an accident), whistle, waterproof over-trousers, snow goggles, spare sweater, scarf, balaclava, torch, food, spare map, basic first aid equipment, toilet paper and drink.

Whistle and torch are important and could save the life of the walker stranded, lost or injured. Steady flashes in the dark will alert search parties. Six blasts on the whistle every minute for regular periods may be heard by the rescue services and result in the cool-headed, well-prepared accident victim being found in freezing fog. Normally the fog-bound walker who comes across a stream should follow it, because all streams on the moors eventually reach a road or habitation.

Winter hill walking without warm clothes, good boots, waterproof gaiters and a tough cagoule that really does keep out wind and rain could be suicidally foolish. Waxed, waterproof mittens are also essential when the temperatures are below zero and rain is freezing on everything. These mittens can be worn comfortably over woollen gloves.

I prefer fleecy lined, woollen stockings, two or three pairs, tied under the knees with strips of crêpe bandage. My heavyweight climbing breeches, which have seen twenty-five years' service, fit comfortably even over long-johns. On my head I usually wear a close-knit woollen ski hat pulled down over the ears. If it is unbearably cold, I'll also put on a balaclava under the cagoule hood.

I never sport dull colours in the winter wilderness. A rescue helicopter can't see a camouflaged body lying beside a tor. My hat is red and so are my gaiters, and my cagoule is blue.

On a few occasions I've chosen to bivouac in a snowhole without a tent, but the experiences weren't enjoyable and an enforced bivouac in arctic conditions is best avoided wherever possible.

There is an element of danger in winter hill walking and to go to remote, snow-covered places without mental, physical and material preparation is stupid. Finally, I always let my family know where I'm going and the route I intend to take. In bad weather Dartmoor is a beautiful death trap. Among the animals it destroys there could be human victims – the unfortunate or the idiotic who set the rescue operations in motion.

The Dartmoor Rescue Group was formed nearly twenty years ago. Now it has four sections: Tavistock, with its extra base section, Okehampton, Plymouth and Ashburton, all of which have highly trained volunteer members. They use sophisticated techniques and can call upon a fund of expertise and local knowledge. Belonging as they do to SARDA (the Search and Rescue Dogs Association), the sections use dogs capable of sniffing out victims buried in the snow and the success rate of the Group is high.

A Section operation, in the wake of a blizzard that had piled immense drifts on the North Moor, emphasised the 'mountain' character of the region. The ice-plastered grass and moss of the mires was bounded by the snow carpet. Whiteness glistened. Snow powder rose from the tors, wavered and vanished. Granite crosses were gaunt and metallic with ice. Light was agitated, like a display of static electricity on the snow.

The operation began with the members arriving by car kitted out for the hills and collecting around the control vehicle for the leader's briefing. They were surrounded by the moor at its most hostile.

Once alerted and briefed the teams moved off into the wilderness to search for casualties. With them went the dog and the dog handler. Information was coming in over the radio. Strange, tinny voices crackled across the ether.

A team in their bright cagoules and back-packs went up the side of the cleave towards the tors on the hill. They searched the area as snow veiled the rocks. Radio messages were exchanged with the control vehicle; but the casualty was in the valley where the river was a conspicuous swarthy ribbon. The dog, a border collie, had the keen, inquisitive nose of a fox. He followed the scent trail over the rocks and found the body in the snow. The barking brought an instant response and radio contact with base.

Between two tors above the cleave, a second team appeared and a party was seen descending the hillside with the rescue stretcher. The teams gathered and the casualty was hauled up the hill on the single-wheeled stretcher to the ridge and taken back to the base vehicle which had summoned the ambulance.

On this occasion the casualty was suffering from hypothermia – induced by exposure to cold weather. It is a curious illness, the 'winter sickness'. The cooling of the body surface and the loss of heat at the body core leave victims cold, weary, sluggish in thought and action, with distorted vision and spasms of shivering. They behave like drunks, staggering and falling over, slurring their speech, occasionally cursing until they collapse into unconsciousness and death.

Survival is a baffling business. Man, who can get to the moon without too much discomfort, can finish up a corpse on Dartmoor in the winter; and while the body is carried off the vole burrows out of the snowdrift into the sun, full of life. The small animal has been equipped by nature to survive where man is always in peril. Creation is forever sending its travellers through time on voyages of evolution while a Dartmoor winter hints at human frailty.

THE FIRESIDE

The Big Freeze continued and muggy, wet weather was recalled with nostalgia by people weary of snow and ice and winds full of malice. Startling images could be quarried out of days spent wandering around the edge of the moors. Brentor Church perched spectacularly on the volcanic outcrop of Brent Tor had become the symbol of all that is remote from the 20th century. As a boy I thought I would find the Holy Grail there. The Devil's Cauldron at Lydford Gorge was ice and roaring white water. Flowers were wilting on Jay's Grave. The snow on the car parks was patterned with the tracks of ponies and sheep and the footprints of birds. The larks were silent and water had stiffened into a hard light.

At lunchtime or in the evening it was good to shake the snow off my boots and settle before a pub fire. The Rugglestone Inn near Widecombe remains one of my favourite pubs because of Audrey's no-nonsense, Devonshire manner which goes with the authentic Twenties parlour and the absence of anything pretentious in the way of drinks and furniture.

The Rock Inn, Haytor Vale, with its big open fire has inspired some hilarious conversations with friends over a madras curry; and I've been grateful on many a cold day for the fire at The Warren House Inn and the hospitality of The Drew Arms at Drewsteignton. The Glebe Hotel at North Bovey has provided sumptuous dinners, and breakfast at The Moorland Hotel, Haytor Vale has never been anything less than generous.

Often when I am at the fireside with my climbing socks steaming and warmth spreading through my body I sift over old times. Outside the storm winds may be blowing but staring through my thoughts I see the April blossom on Joe White's cider apple trees at Batworthy and Dave French, the water bailiff, peering at the salmon at their redds in the Cherry Brook.

Looking back even further to primary school days I am racing down Widecombe

Aunt Mable Mudge, landlady of The Drew Arms, Drewsteignton, for over 60 years.

Hill on my bike or trekking up the Swincombe for my first sight of merlins. Climbing Hay Tor and the Dewerstone; swimming in Haytor Quarry Ponds or shooting the torrents in the Newbridge Valley; coming up the East Dart to Cranmere Pool in pursuit of Henry Williamson's *Tarka*; bivouacking in the holly-tree cave at Greator Rocks; walking for miles and miles under blue skies – so many times the wilderness has enriched my life. The salmon fisherman, the old Master of Foxhounds whom I like and respect, despite our differing views on hunting, farmers, stone wallers, water bailiffs, monks, quarrymen, literary gents and artists, naturalists, Ordnance Survey people, National Park Rangers, fellow walkers encountered at Fur Tor or somewhere almost as remote, innkeepers and various eccentrics – these have added something to the wilderness experience. Love of the place is the common bond.

Once, back in the Fifties, I met an elderly lady in rubber boots, headscarf and overcoat struggling to do a watercolour sketch of Fox Tor. The air was grey with the impending snow and it was dark by the time I had escorted her back to Princetown where she told me she had intended working until the light failed! Then there was the night crossing of the moor, North to South by moonlight, when I was young and time or distance weren't important.

I had roughly thirty miles to cover and all night to do it in provided my compass reading and the moon did not let me down. It was summer and the air warm and the sky cloudless. Leaving Belstone I followed the East Okement to its source on the North Mire. For a while, loneliness lifted in me on a squirt of panic and for the first time on Dartmoor I craved company. My mind raced ahead to Two Bridges and the hotel. Human warmth was infinitely preferable to the bogs and tors that held the wetness of moonlight. But at length my mood changed and soon I was striding along on the edge of elation. The star dance and the moon were glorious and I was as fit as the butcher's dog.

Nightwalking had me using my eyes and ears and nose like an animal. I didn't hurry although I lost my way a couple of times. Beyond Peat Cot I found the desolation of the South Moor exhilarating, despite the hazards of the mires. After Cator's Beam I wanted to come down between the rivers Erme and Avon. Occasional encounters with

The stone circle on Scorhill Down.

sheep and ponies brought me up sharp but I was absolutely content and wide awake. Eventually on Ugborough Common near South Brent and journey's end I unrolled my sleeping bag because I wanted to finish the walk at sunrise.

Gazing up at the sky I have never felt closer to Nature or my own kind.

At the pub fireside I frequently read William Crossing, the author of *Ancient Stone Crosses of Dartmoor and its Boderland, Amid Devonia's Alps, Gems in a Granite Setting, A Hundred Years on Dartmoor, Folk Rhymes of Devon, From a Dartmoor Cot* and the great classic – *Guide to Dartmoor.*

Crossing opened the door on many mysteries which puzzled me when I was young. From him I learnt that the Forest of Dartmoor wasn't a big, tree-covered place. It is in Lydford Parish in the centre of the moors and kings used to hunt there.

Surrounding the Forest are the Commons which belong to individual owners, although the land is subject to certain traditional rights of other people.

Crossing's work constitutes more than an encyclopaedic knowledge of the granite upland with its rivers, mires, tors and in-country. He evokes atmosphere, over and over again. The wilderness struck a chord in the man and his accuracy of description and observation sprang from a lifetime's experience of the moor's weather moods and the landscape and man's presence. Dartmoor was his heart-place.

William Crossing was born on November 14th 1847 at Plymouth and died on September 2nd 1928. Earning a living as a writer for newspapers like *The Western Morning News* proved hard and he was always struggling to make ends meet. Yet his enthusiasm for Dartmoor was never blunted by personal hardship. Seated comfortably in front of the blaze I thumb through part three of *The Western Morning News Guide to Dartmoor* that came out in five parts in 1914. It is a small paperback volume with faded green covers and old fashioned typeset; and it sold for six old pence. Every time I open it nostalgia for Crossing's Dartmoor begins to churn in my stomach.

From our different compartments of time, Crossing and I have sat on Rippon Tor in the snow, looking down over the white countryside as if the years separating his winter and my winter were no further removed from each other than dusk is from dawn. Recently I was there under the snow clouds, alive to the wind and cold, as he had been all those decades ago. Yet I felt his presence strongly on Holwell Lawn where lapwings were crying. The bird calls brought elements of Edwardian Dartmoor into focus: damp homespun tweed, walking sticks and knapsacks, dusty tracks, chickens on the road, mulled cider and walkers striding along in their pure wool, smoke-tan waterproofs.

Wherever one goes on the moors the past is waiting.

THE PARABLE OF THE LAMB

By mid-March much of the snow had gone off the Dartmoor fields. The sun coming out established the white and green in marvellous counterpoint. Against the hedges were the rain-pocked ruins of the drifts. Gatherings of magpies were feeding on the wet pastures. Out of the wind the sun was quite warm and everywhere the snow was melting and the mud had softened to a porridgy consistency; but the thaw had come too late for many birds and animals.

The lambing was underway at the farm on the west side of the moor. Mist pressed down and from all around the field rose the low contented grunting of the ewes and the urgent cries of their young. It was profoundly moving. One ewe was in the corner of the pasture on the point of dropping her lamb. The head of the little creature was showing but, despite the mother sitting down to push, there were no signs of imminent delivery. The ewe pawed the ground and panted and then pushed once more. Across the pasture came the farmer and his wife and with their assistance the lamb was born.

For me that birth said everything there is to say about the husbandry of compassion. It is extraordinary that a creature like a sheep, with man's help, can come through a hard winter carrying fresh life in her body. And the moor had also carried life within itself during the cold dark months and as the earth rolled towards the sun it was beginning to show. In Nature all things keep their bargain with birth but Dartmoor supplies a broad, bare stage for the triumph of resurrection.

When I walk towards the hills, the horizons retreat and reassemble beyond. Each season colours that mystery and brings something of value within my reach. Standing on Fur Tor at the centre of an immense solitude I'm reminded that this is one of those priceless gems of upland Britain which we should never seek to plunder for our amusement or financial gain. Mistakes have been made but hopefully, too, lessons have been learnt. Preserving Dartmoor should be of paramount importance.

As the flight into mediocrity becomes a stampede, an increasing number of spirits will turn towards this refuge to confront Nature on Nature's terms.

Therefore, the birth of a lamb in a cold moorland field and celandines sharing the hedge bank with snow are an affirmation of hope. Much that I value is manifested in this transition. The seasons change as the year travels its full cycle; but the cycle is continuous and so is life. It goes on and on. Individuals arrive and depart but the inextinguishable force is there all the time feeding on what the living world has to give it.

The lambing at the end of winter represents this tremendous festival that begins with birth and never ends.

INDEX